BY ROBERTO CALASSO

I. The Ruin of Kasch

II. The Marriage of Cadmus and Harmony

III. Ka

IV. K.

V. Tiepolo Pink

VI. La Folie Baudelaire

VII. Ardor

VIII. The Celestial Hunter

IX. The Unnamable Present

The Art of the Publisher

The Forty-nine Steps

Literature and the Gods

THE
UNNAMABLE
PRESENT

THE
UNNAMABLE
PRESENT

⟨ⅲⅲ⟩

ROBERTO
CALASSO

TRANSLATED FROM THE ITALIAN
BY RICHARD DIXON

FARRAR, STRAUS AND GIROUX
NEW YORK

Farrar, Straus and Giroux
175 Varick Street, New York 10014

Copyright © 2017 by Adelphi Edizioni S.p.A. Milano
Translation copyright © 2019 by Richard Dixon
All rights reserved
Printed in the United States of America
Originally published in Italian in 2017 by Adelphi Edizioni,
Italy, as *L'innominabile attuale*
English translation published in the United States by
Farrar, Straus and Giroux
First American edition, 2019

Library of Congress Cataloging-in-Publication Data
Names: Calasso, Roberto, author. | Dixon, Richard, translator.
Title: The unnamable present / Roberto Calasso ; translated from the
    Italian by Richard Dixon.
Other titles: Innominabile attuale. English
Description: First American edition. | New York : Farrar, Straus and
    Giroux, [2019] | "Originally published in Italian in 2017 by Adelphi
    Edizioni, Italy, as L'innominabile attuale" —Title verso. | Includes
    bibliographical references and index.
Identifiers: LCCN 2018041577 | ISBN 9780374279479 (hardcover)
Subjects: LCSH: Civilization, Modern—20th century. | Civilization,
    Modern—21st century. | Intellectual life—History—20th century. |
    World War, 1939–1945—Influence.
Classification: LCC CB358 .C3313 2019 | DDC 909.82—dc23
LC record available at https://lccn.loc.gov/2018041577

Designed by Jonathan D. Lippincott

Our books may be purchased in bulk for promotional, educational,
or business use. Please contact your local bookseller or the Macmillan
Corporate and Premium Sales Department at 1-800-221-7945, extension
5442, or by e-mail at MacmillanSpecialMarkets@macmillan.com.

www.fsgbooks.com
www.twitter.com/fsgbooks • www.facebook.com/fsgbooks

1   3   5   7   9   10   8   6   4   2

CONTENTS

I. TOURISTS AND TERRORISTS   1

II. THE VIENNA GAS COMPANY   91

III. SIGHTING OF THE TOWERS   165

Notes   *169*

Index   *187*

I

TOURISTS AND TERRORISTS

For we who are living at this moment, the most exact and most acute sensation is one of not knowing where we are treading from day to day. The ground is brittle, lines blur, materials fray, prospects waver. Then we realize more clearly than before that we are living in the "unnamable present."

In the years between 1933 and 1945 the world made a partially successful attempt at self-destruction. What came after was shapeless, rough, and overpowerful. In this new millennium, it is shapeless, rough, and ever more powerful. Elusive in every single aspect, the opposite of the world that Hegel had sought to grasp in the grip of concept. Even for scientists it is a shattered world. It has no style of its own but uses every style.

This state of things may even seem exciting. But it excites only sectarians, convinced that they hold the key to what is going on. The others—most—have to adapt. They follow the advertising. Taoist fluidity is the least common virtue. One is continually assailed by the contours of an object that nobody has ever managed to see in its entirety. This is the *normal world.*

The Age of Anxiety was the title W. H. Auden gave to a long poem for several voices, set in a New York bar toward the end of World War II. Today those voices sound remote, as though they came from another valley. There's no shortage of anxiety but it no longer prevails. What prevails is a ubiquitous lack of substance, a deadly insubstantiality. It is the age of the insubstantial.

Terror is founded on the idea that only killing guarantees meaning. All else seems feeble, uncertain, inadequate. On that foundation are built the various motivations used to justify the act of terror. And connected also to that foundation, in an obscure way that involves a metaphysical element, is blood sacrifice. As if, from age to age and in widely different places, there were some compelling and irrepressible need to perform killings that might otherwise seem gratuitous and unreasonable. An ominous mirror-like resemblance between the origins and the present today. A hexed mirror.

Islamic terrorism is sacrificial: in its perfect form, the victim is the bomber. Those who are killed in the attack are the beneficial *fruit* of the killer's sacrifice. At one time, the fruit of the sacrifice was invisible. The whole ritual machine was conceived to establish contact and interchange between the visible and the invisible. Now, instead, the fruit of the sacrifice has become visible, measurable, photographable. Like missiles, the sacrificial attack is aimed at the sky, but falls to earth. And so there's a prevalence of attacks by suicide bombers who blow themselves up. Or in any event, the attackers are expected to end up getting killed. Setting off some remotely controlled explosion obfuscates the sacrificial nature of the attack.

The prime enemy of Islamic terrorism is the *secular world*, preferably in its collective forms: tourism, entertainment, offices, museums, bars, department stores, public transport. The fruit of the sacrifice will not just be many killings, but will have a wider effect. Like every sacrificial practice, Islamic terrorism is founded on *meaning*. And that meaning is interlinked with other meanings, all converging on the same motive: a hatred of secular society.

In the latest stage of its formation, Islamic terrorism coincides with the spread of online pornography in the 1990s. What had always been dreamt of and desired was suddenly there to be seen, easily and always available. At the same time it tore away the whole structure of their rules relating to sex. If that negation was possible, *everything* had to be possible. The secular world had invaded their mind with something irresistible, which attracted them and at the same time mocked and undermined them. Without the use of weapons—and, moreover, without assuming or needing the presence of meaning. But they would go *further*. And beyond sex, there is only death. A death stamped with meaning.

Since the time of Sergey Nechayev we have known that terror can take other paths. It was then called *nihilistic terror*. Today an alternative version of it can be conceived: *secular terror*. Understood as a simple procedure, available therefore for all kinds of fundamentalism, which would each give it a specific coloring for their own ends. Or for individuals, who can thus give vent to their own obsessions.

The power that stirs terrorism and makes it so vexing is not the power of religion, or politics, or economics, or the furtherance of some cause. It is the power of chance. Terrorism exposes the hitherto untarnished power that rules everything and lays bare its foundation. At the same time it is an eloquent way of revealing the immense expanse of all that surrounds society and ignores it. Society had to reach the point of feeling self-sufficient and supreme before chance could emerge as its principal antagonist and persecutor.

Secular terror first seeks to escape from its sacrificial compulsion. To cross to pure murder. The result of the operation has to seem totally fortuitous and scattered in anonymous corners. It will then seem clear that chance is the ultimate sponsor of these acts. What is more frightening: the significant killing or the casual killing? Answer: the casual killing. Because chance is more widespread than significance. In front of significant killing, what is insignificant can feel protected by its own insignificance. But in front of the casual killing, what is insignificant finds itself particularly vulnerable, precisely because of its own insignificance. In the end, terror no longer needs a collective instigator. Instigator and perpetrator can be one and the same person. He can be a solitary individual, no less than a state or a sect, obeying one self-imposed commandment: to kill.

Significant terrorism is not the ultimate but the penultimate form of terrorism. The ultimate is *casual* terrorism, the form of terrorism that most corresponds to the *god of the moment.*

In its first issue of September 2016, *Rumiyah* ("Rome"), the ISIS multilingual online magazine that replaced *Dābiq*, indicated the path of casual terrorism in an article titled "The Kafir's Blood Is Halal for You, So Shed It." And it delved into detail, offering a prime list of possible targets: "The businessman riding to work in a taxicab, the young adults (post-pubescent 'children') engaged in sports activities in the park, and the old man waiting in line to buy a sandwich. Indeed, even the blood of the kafir street vendor selling flowers to those passing by is *halal*." There are no distinctions of class or age, except for the case of the young athlete, who must be post-pubescent.

The figure of the suicide killer is certainly not a recent invention. In Islam, it began with Hasan-i Sabbah, the "Old Man of the Mountain" of whom Marco Polo writes, a figure whose legend grew around that of the Ismailite strategist who for years had hatched conspiracies from the fortress of Alamut. According to contemporary sources he was strict, austere, cruel, and reclusive. According to Marshall Hodgson, the most authoritative historian on the sect: "He is said to have remained continuously within his house, writing and directing operations—as it is always put, during all those years he went only twice out of his house, and twice onto the roof." Meanwhile, envoys of the Old Man of the Mountain, scattered around the Seljuk kingdom that

Hasan-i Sabbah was seeking to destroy, killed powerful men, generally with daggers, before getting themselves killed. They were *fida'iyyan*, "those who sacrifice themselves" or "assassins," a word that meant "consumers of hashish," as Paul Pelliot has definitively proved.

Two centuries later, when the fortress of Alamut was a ruin, destroyed a few years before by the Mongols of Hulagu Khan, and the *sect of the Assassins* was just a memory, someone told Marco Polo the story of the Old Man of the Mountain. Odoric of Pordenone would repeat it, unvaried, several years later.

According to both, the Old Man of the Mountain "had made, in a valley between two mountains, the most beautiful and the largest garden in the world." And "in it were noble youths and damsels, the most beautiful in the world, who best knew how to sing and play and dance. And the Old Man had them believe that this was paradise." But there was one condition: "In this garden no one entered except those he wanted to be an assassin."

When the Old Man chose to send someone on a mission, he made him fall into a drugged stupor and sent him away from the garden. "And when the Old Man wants to have any person killed, he chooses the one who is strongest, and has him kill the one he wishes. And they do so willingly, so as to return to paradise . . . And in this way no man survives before the Old Man of the Mountain, if he so wishes it; and I tell you he causes dread among many kings for that fear."

The Old Man of the Mountain had given his guests the

taste of paradise. Centuries later, it would be enough to offer the assurance that paradise is reserved for martyrs of the *jihad* and is brimming with pleasures, as is written in the Koran. But first it was necessary to discover the *pleasure of death*.

The Old Man of the Mountain, as he appears in Joinville and other medieval chronicles, was a well-known and legendary presence, like Prester John. It was assumed the reader knew who he was. But it was clearer to Nietzsche than to anyone else. "When the Christian Crusades fought with that invincible order of Assassins, that order of free spirits *par excellence*, whose lowest grades lived in an obedience such as no monastic order has ever attained, they managed to get some inkling of that symbol and that motto carved on wood, which was reserved only for the highest grades, as their *secretum*: 'Nothing is true, everything is allowed' . . . Well now, *this* was spiritual *freedom*, in this way belief in truth itself was *cancelled* . . . Has a European, Christian free spirit ever managed to *lose itself* in this proposition and its *labyrinthine* consequences?"

"Nothing is true, everything is allowed": where had Nietzsche read that fateful phrase? In *Geschichte der Assassinen*, a dense, ambitious, and invaluable work, published just after the Congress of Vienna and unanimously disparaged by later Islamologists, Joseph von Hammer-Purgstall had written: "*That nothing is true and everything is allowed* remained the foundation of the secret doctrine, which was communicated, however, to very few and hidden under the veil of the strictest religiosity and devotion, all the more since worldly submission and self-sacrifice were sanctioned with a reward of eternal glorification."

The epigraph to Betty Bouthoul's *Le Vieux de la Montagne*, a book from which William S. Burroughs found his obsession for Hasan-i Sabbah, contains a few lines from Nicolas de Staël, who had killed himself three years earlier: "Murder and suicide, inseparable and so distant at first view . . .

"Murder, projected shadow of suicide, which incessantly blur like two clouds that are immaterial and atrociously alive . . .

"To kill getting killed . . ."

Conspiracy is born with history. So also the phantom of a hidden center that governs events. Suicide attackers are traced back to Osama bin Laden in the caves of Tora Bora, who is traced back to Hasan-i Sabbah in the fortress of Alamut. There are some forms that don't die out. They change, they become filled and emptied of meaning according to the circumstances. But one subtle thread always binds them to their origins.

Nature has come at least once to the assistance of those seeking to impose the universal rule of the *shari'a*, opening the way without even the use of terrorism. In December 2004, the province of Aceh, on the tip of Sumatra, was struck by a tsunami that destroyed everything and left just one mosque standing. It meant starting again from nothing, a situation that every utopia yearned for. And so an enclave of the *shari'a* has been set up. Its conspicuous custodians are the Guardians of Virtue: "They have green Islamic uniforms, Malacca whips and hearts of stone. They come from the countryside and know exactly how to treat the people of the city. At Banda Aceh they are usually to be seen on a Friday, before prayers. They go round with a megaphone and a pickup truck, also of greenish color, on which are the words Wilayatul Hisbah: *shari'a* patrol. They are not many, a dozen, but they turn up more or less anywhere and when you're not expecting it." They comb the cafés, public gardens, roads, bedrooms. Arrests and punishments are immediate. Canings performed in the public square.

Islamic terrorism regards a Coptic church or a Scandinavian department store as targets that are equally appropriate. The sole need is to demonstrate a rejection of the West in every aspect, from Christianity to Secularity, by an organism far cruder than the West itself. The hatred has to be concentrated in one place, ideally somewhere teeming with life. But that resentment is not new. It already existed fifty years ago. Why only now does it take on such forms? A theorist of the Web would immediately say it is one of the many results of *disintermediation*. And of the fact that the world is tending to become *instantaneous* and *simultaneous*. Those who kill themselves while killing others are a supreme model of disintermediation.

At the close of the millennium, in Islamic countries throughout almost the whole world, people could access in just a few seconds a limitless number of images of naked women performing sexual acts. It was a source of both extreme outrage and irresistible attraction, more than in other countries. And it was also a powerful incentive for any kind of acting out.

Sayyid Qutb docked at New York in November 1948, appalled by a young half-dressed woman who had knocked on his cabin door asking for hospitality. He was a government official from Cairo who had come to America on a scholarship to study English. He observed America as he moved from place to place, then settled in Greeley, Colorado, which seemed at first like a paradise. But he soon had second thoughts and roundly condemned the American way of life, especially after certain Sunday evening parties he had attended when college refectories were closed and foreign students would go to various churches where, after the service, there was food and people sometimes danced. They dimmed the lights and Qutb saw legs straying ("naked," he added), arms draped around waists, chests swaying—and a song played from an Esther Williams movie. Enough was enough.

Back in Egypt, Qutb was soon a leading political figure. When Gamal Abdel Nasser came to power, he appointed him head of the Editorial Committee for the Revolution. But it didn't last long. In Egypt then, as later in Algeria, there were only two paths: either military or the *shari'a*, supported by the Muslim Brotherhood. And Qutb represented the latter. In 1954 he ended up in prison, was then released, and was invited to run the magazine of the Muslim Brotherhood. This too was short-lived. He was rearrested. He was often ill and had to be moved to the prison hospital, where he spent ten years, during which he wrote an eight-volume commentary on the Koran. But his incendiary work was *Milestones*, whose manuscript was dispatched little by little from prison. The book provided instructions for the "advance guard," who had to conquer the world in the name of Islam by rescuing it from *jahiliyyah*, from the pernicious "ignorance" shared by those Muslims who didn't obey the *shari'a* and by all other living people. This guided the actions of another Egyptian, Ayman al-Zawahiri, and his comrade Osama bin Laden, as well as the man who would later become Ayatollah Khamenei.

Qutb was once again released. The authorities were now prepared to let him leave the country. But Qutb consistently refused. He was eventually put on trial and sentenced to death. One of the three judges of the tribunal was Anwar Sadat. When the sentence was read out, Qutb said: "I performed *jihad* for fifteen years until I earned this martyrdom, *shahadah*." He was hanged at dawn on August 29, 1966.

If so many human tribes have celebrated sacrifices in so many different places and ways, there must be some deep reason for it. Indeed, a tangle of reasons that can never be unraveled. The secular world has certainly never approved of the celebration of sacrifices. But this was one aspect of the past from which it didn't know how to free itself. One look at Karl Kraus's *The Last Days of Mankind*, much of which reports what newspapers were writing and what was being heard in the streets, is enough to confirm that during World War I people were talking as much about "sacrifices" as about military action. But that wasn't enough. There had to be another war—and, within it, a vast and horrifying operation of disinfestation, once again to pay off the sacrifice. But even this was not enough. After centuries of quiescence, during which it seemed to have lost its spirit, as if it had been sapped by the wonder of its earlier bloom, something within Islam had been roused. From the mouth of Sayyid Qutb came a call for new "healthy values" to counter the corruption of the West and the confounding of Islam itself, caused above all by a gradual yielding to Western ways of life. So some began to kill themselves, in small numbers, in order to kill many others, in the greatest number possible.

The heredity of sacrifice had to result in something: this something was two great wars, then the excess of armed power prevented further advance. Terrorism then took over: sporadic, ubiquitous, incessant killings, performed ever more casually, which keep the sacrificial fire alive. It is an exact reverse of Vedic doctrines. But none of those who act are aware of this. Like automata, they operate in a workshop that has two departments: one heavenly and one infernal.

Sacrifice and terrorism converge in one most delicate point: the choice of victim. In sacrifice, the model victim will be one of unblemished integrity, of particular beauty—or otherwise an ordinary, interchangeable, multipliable being. In terrorism it can be someone in power—or otherwise it can be anyone who happens to be in a certain place at a certain moment.

There are two divergent and coexistent paths: election and condemnation. And two realms: grace and chance, irreducible powers. The ways in which they superimpose, merge, separate produce countless consequences of the most subtle, the most incisive kind: consequences that affect everything else, whose only common feature is the act of killing.

To understand the transformations that sacrifice has undergone in the secular age, *sacrifice* has to be swapped for the word *experiment*. Which is not only what happens every day in laboratories—and this would already indicate its immensity. But experimentation is what society performs every day on itself. And here the ambivalence of the word becomes even clearer, for the two supreme social experimenters of the twentieth century were Hitler and Stalin. It is no coincidence that Stalin invoked the "engineers of human souls." But they were more like certain ruthless lobotomizers, acting always in the name of science. All ravagers of the unknown.

The twentieth century saw the crystallization of a process of enormous significance, which has affected all that goes under the name "religious." Secular society, without any need for proclamations, has become the ultimate repository for all meaning, almost as if its form corresponded to the physiology of whatever community, and meaning had only to be sought within society itself. Which itself can assume the most divergent political and economic forms, whether capitalist or socialist, democratic or dictatorial, protectionist or free-trading, military or sectarian. All to be considered, in every case, as mere variants of a single entity: society itself. It is as though, after millennia, imagination had been stripped of its capacity to look *beyond* society in search of something that gives meaning to what is going on *within* society. An extremely bold step, which involves a formidable easing of the mind. Yet this is always short-lasting. To live "beyond good and evil" is something that meets insurmountable resistance. To produce—or at least to favor—that easing of the mind is a crucial characteristic of democracy. But one that it cannot maintain.

Compared with all other regimes, democracy is not a specific idea, but a series of procedures that claim to be capable of accommodating all ideas, except those that seek to overthrow democracy itself. And this is its most vulnerable point, as Germany demonstrated in January 1933. Secular society has thus shown itself quick and able to reabsorb within itself, under false colors, those same powers that it had just expelled. Theology ended up being transformed into politics, while theology itself was relegated to universities.

But the process is applied at all levels: without the thrill of the numinous, secular society refuses to exist, even if *numinous* is a word allowed only in academic circles. Since it cannot name that which it worships according to the rules of a canon, society appears condemned to a new and elusive superstition: the superstition of itself, the most difficult to perceive and to dispel. So it has happened that the worst disasters have come to light when secular societies have sought to become *organic*, a recurrent aspiration among all societies that develop the cult of themselves. Always with the best intentions. Always to regain a lost unity and supposed harmony. Marx and Rousseau, but also Hitler and Lenin, as well as the productivist Henri de Saint-Simon, have all found short-lasting agreement on this. *Organic* is fine, for everyone. No one dares to say that the deprecated atomization of society can also be a form of self-defense from more serious ills. It is easier to hide in an atomized society. No one expects the secret police to knock on their door at four in the morning.

All of this has happened as the result of a long, painful evolution that has continued uninterrupted—even though at times it has been hidden. If we had to determine some starting point for such a process—a date that can only be arbitrary, chosen for purely illustrative purposes—no image would be more fitting than that of Sparta as Jacob Burckhardt described it, concentrating the essential into a few words with his usual sober style: "On the earth, power can have a noble mission; perhaps on it alone, on a territory protected by it, can civilizations of a higher order emerge. But the power of Sparta seems to have appeared to the world almost only for itself and for its own success, and its constant pathos was the enslavement of submissive populations and the extension of its dominion as an end in itself."

These words of Burckhardt have a particular importance and are applicable not just to Sparta but to recent history and to what is happening today, as is shown by a curious circumstance regarding their publication. In 1940, the Deutsche Buch-Gemeinschaft published Burckhardt's *Griechische Kulturgeschichte* in a single volume, prefacing it with a note signed "The Publisher" which stated: "The scientific padding, notes, source references, as well as certain repetitions and details that interest only the academic, have been eliminated. In this way the work has been made more readable." Well, having reached page 50, the reader may notice that a whole paragraph has been omitted—and it was one that ended with the words quoted above. But we should also read the lines before it, which were also suppressed: "It has already been noted above how generally costly the foundation of a city would be. But the foundation of Sparta in particular was extremely costly to the subjugated populations. They were given the choice of all types of slavery, annihilation, deportation." And Burckhardt concluded that, even if such a social setup had its own grandeur, one couldn't avoid looking upon it "without any sympathy." For a German publisher loyal to the regime (and by then they were all loyal to the regime) it was intolerable that certain facts be mentioned with such inflexible precision and "without any sympathy," as Burckhardt declared.

We might ask whether secular society believes in anything other than itself. Or has it reached that noble degree of wisdom at which people stop believing, but limit themselves to observing, studying, understanding, in an undefined and unpredictable progression? Well, this condition, which requires a lucid and concentrated mind, doesn't seem to correspond with what is happening every day in the vast secular society that has now spread across all continents and is continually racked by troubles of varying origin—troubles reminiscent of those that took place in times of religious war. Yet those wars were based on conflicts of belief. Invisible armies of theologies and liturgies fought alongside earthly forces. Today, however, it would be impossible to find such armies. The conflicts of society are no longer aimed at something that lies beyond and above it, but at society itself. Which is above all a vast terrain over which to intervene, a laboratory where opposing forces try in turn to exert control over the experiments.

This picture ought to be enough for us to recognize that secular society has a unique character. Every ethnographer of the positivist school knew that the hundreds of societies catalogued by his discipline had at least one feature in common: that of believing in powers and entities outside society itself, which were invisible, self-sufficient, and loomed over the life of everyone. Yet secular society— which might otherwise be called *experimental society*, thereby isolating its specific characteristic—declares that it can do without them.

But when and how did this singular configuration come about? If it is true that its first symptoms can be found, each time with valid arguments, in a period ranging between the Paleolithic Age and the French Revolution, there is always a moment of crystallization in which the complete figure emerges. And in this case it could be identified as what we might call the age of Bouvard and Pécuchet. These two intrepid innovators, misunderstood even today, were the first total experimenters. No area of human activity remained closed to them. And in every direction their investigations, whether on gardening or astrophysics, left indelible traces. Their endeavor was to prepare the field for all future experimentation, which had to be founded however on a sort of all-inclusive encyclopedia. In them can be found the embryonic form of what would one day be called the Internet. But if Bouvard and Pécuchet can rightly be called the founding heroes of experimental society, there is always a guidebook for what relates to doctrine, such as the letters of Saint Paul for Christianity, or Stalin's brief *History of the Communist (Bolshevik) Party of the Soviet Union* for Soviet communism, or Freud's *The Interpretation of Dreams* for psychoanalysis. For anthropology, it was Émile Durkheim's *Les Formes élémentaires de la vie religieuse*, published in 1912.

By a curious paradox, Durkheim's book looked the exact opposite of an essay his nephew Marcel Mauss had published thirteen years before. Mauss and Henri Hubert had written on "the nature and the function of sacrifice"— and Mauss, like a Vedic seer in disguise, was interested above all in describing the essential features of the "nature" of sacrifice, while not overlooking its social "function." Mauss wanted to find out what sacrifice is, what risks it brings, with what it makes contact. Durkheim, on the other hand, was interested only in "function": that singular phenomenon by which abstruse and vertiginous ceremonies served to preserve the balance and cohesion of a society. Indeed, of any society.

Durkheim's approach won the day—and it still remains an undisputed foundation. Indeed, anthropology today, whatever its methods or schools, either is functionalist or it doesn't exist. This is the common, universally accepted, ground of thought. But could it be any different? As a study *of* society, anthropology can only offer itself as the *locus electionis* where that supreme superstition which is society itself is acted out.

The basis for the superstition of society is set out in Durkheim's main work with formidable candor, unequaled clarity, and with absolutely no fear about reaching extreme conclusions. Durkheim was well aware that, in his theory, no conceptual dividing line could be drawn between the Arunta tribes that celebrate the rites of the witchetty grub "imitating the movements of the animal when it leaves the chrysalis and struggles to take flight," and the austere frock-coated officials around him who praised the wonders of Progress and Science. Each of them were branches of a single, dense tree. Both were cases of "deliria," if we choose to use the word Durkheim himself felt most appropriate. But they were eminently useful deliria, for it was only thanks to them that social cohesion was assured, among Arunta tribesmen as much as in Third Republic France. And here Durkheim gave way to tones of astringent eloquence: "In summing up, we must say that society is by no means the illogical or alogical, inconsistent and fantastic being that people too often like to imagine. On the contrary, collective consciousness is the highest form of psychic life, for it is a consciousness of consciousnesses. Being placed outside of and above individual and local contingencies, it sees things only in their permanent and essential aspect, which it crystallizes into communicable ideas. And since it sees from above, it sees far ahead; at every moment of time, it embraces all known reality; that is why it alone can furnish the mind with terms that are applicable to the totality of beings and make it possible to think of them."

This reads like a pre-Socratic who is referring to *lógos*. And yet he is the founder of that "dismal science" called sociology. But there is always a founder before the founder. And Durkheim himself described Saint-Simon as the "founder of sociology." What did they have in common? They didn't just study and analyze something that was called "society." They were the first priests—more lucid and consistent than others who stopped halfway—of a new cult: the cult of the deified society. At one time it was enough to deify the emperor to ensure social cohesion. This was no longer enough. Society itself had to be deified. And cohesion became the divine substance coursing through its body. Durkheim was not interested in criticizing (or demonstrating the nonexistence of) the (divine) object that religious men claimed they turned to. On the contrary, with paternal solicitude he reassured them: that object exists. But there is no need to give it names of gods, or of one god. That object is society itself: "It is to its members what a god is to his worshippers."

The *ideal type* of anthropologist or ancient historian of today is marked, as Durkheim had hoped, by a distinct lack of interest in those entities whom the officiants claimed were the recipients of the sacrifices. Those entities may be gods, demons, spirits, powers, ancestors: whatever they may be, it is assumed that, since they don't exist, the fact of turning to them is basically no different from addressing a cupboard. What is actually said to the cupboard is regarded as being more or less irrelevant, whereas meticulous attention is given to the economic and structural reasons that might have induced that behavior. And the preferred solution will be that of anyone who succeeds in a detailed description of the homeostatic function that such behavior, aberrant in itself, performs within a given society.

One lone voice in the twentieth century recognized, with clarity and inflexibility, the process that led society into becoming the principal and most powerful of superstitions at work today: that of Simone Weil. Taking Plato's passage in *Republic* that refers to the "big animal," Weil circumscribes in luminous words the phenomenon by which the social "imitates the religious up to the point of becoming one with it, barring a supernatural discernment." It is a discernment that puts reasoning severely to the test, as Weil herself suggests in a comment in brackets: "This mystery creates an apparent kinship between the social and the supernatural, and to a certain extent justifies Durkheim." That "kinship" is an understandable and fatal mistake, if it is true—as Weil writes elsewhere—that, "in many ways, the social is the only idol." A question, then, inevitably arises: how can people today escape from this variant of black magic? How can people in a secular society, trained to ignore the invisible, go back to recognizing it? In what form? What will happen to them if they don't want to stick to one belief, as happens in the pitiful case of those Western sects that describe themselves as Hindu or Buddhist or Shiite or generically Shamanic? A ludicrous game, just one of the various opportunities offered by secular so-ciety and branded with its seal.

The availability of, and access to, all the beliefs of the past is one of the characteristics of an era I used to call *post-historic*. But, if we exclude that inevitably parodistic path, what other possibility remains? Will the anonymous secular subject have to be satisfied with the elision of the invisible, which has now become a precondition of everyday life? This is the watershed. If the essential factor is not belief but knowledge, as every gnosis presupposes, it will be a matter of forging one's way through darkness, using whatever means, in a sort of continual *bricolage* of knowledge, with-out any certainty as to the starting point or any notion of the ultimate destination.

This is the condition, both wretched and exhilarating, faced by those today who belong to no religious denomina-tion but who at the same time refuse to accept the religion—or, more precisely, the superstition—of society. It is a difficult path, which has no name, no points of reference, other than those that are coded and strictly personal. But it is also a path along which one encounters the unexpected assistance of kindred voices, as in a clandestine constella-tion. I don't believe we can expect any more, for the mo-ment. And yet this, if we look carefully, is much indeed. And it is a *great game*, one that many have practiced unob-trusively over the centuries, and one that cannot now avoid the audacity of showing itself in full light. As we read in Wittgenstein's *Remarks on Frazer's Golden Bough*: "One could almost say that man is a ceremonial animal."

Mandelstam thought in pictures and abbreviations. Once, in an essay of 1922, he sketched out in a few words the overwhelming event that was taking place, which no one could name, and to which he himself would become one of the countless victims: society that uses everybody as building material. For what? For society itself. "There are epochs which maintain that man is insignificant, that man is to be used like bricks or mortar, that man should be used for building things, not vice-versa—that things be built for man. Social architecture is measured against the scale of man. Sometimes it may turn against man to enhance its own grandeur by feeding on his humiliation and insignificance." And suddenly the picture emerged: "Everyone senses the monumentality of the forms of social architecture now approaching. The mountain is not yet visible, but it is already casting its shadow over us, and we who have grown accustomed to the monumental forms of social life, who have been trained in the governmental-juridical flatness of the nineteenth century, move in this shadow fearful and bewildered, uncertain whether this is the wing of approaching night or the shadow of our native city which we must enter." Soon after, Mandelstam would be certain; it was indeed "the wing of approaching night"—and he would soon vanish beneath that wing.

"Our age," wrote Henry Kissinger, "is insistently, at times almost desperately, in pursuit of a concept of world order." The Vedics would have translated "world order" as *ṛta*, which also—indissolubly—means "truth." "World order," for Kissinger, means an equilibrium between individual societies, an ideal planetary application of the Peace of Westphalia; for the Vedics it meant "cosmic order," therefore of society and of all that lies outside it and feeds it, therefore of the powers on which every life depends. To find a *world order* by ignoring all that lies outside society can only be a desperate undertaking, even if for reasons quite different from those that Kissinger allows.

"Order" doesn't stand alone, as the Vedics already knew. Kissinger himself recognized this: "Order and freedom, sometimes described as opposite poles on the spectrum of experience, should instead be understood as interdependent." But *freedom* is a word about which the world has not even a vague, general agreement. In a variegated swath of countries that stretches from Morocco to Indonesia, inhabited by one and a half billion people, it is certainly not understood in the way that Kissinger would have it. The freedom of the *shariʿa* is not compatible with that of the Founding Fathers. In such places *order*, which is innately fragile and precarious, could not be "interdependent" with something else, except with the *policing of virtue*, as in Afghanistan or Indonesia.

Henry Kissinger began his career with a hefty book on the Congress of Vienna. Moving from academia to politics, he tried in every way to apply what he called "Westphalian" politics, based on the principle of the balance of powers introduced in the Treaty of Westphalia of 1648 and ultimately reformulated in 1815 with the Congress of Vienna. And, so long as there was a polar opposition between the USA and USSR, that principle found a further corollary, directed this time at nuclear deterrence and dividing up areas of influence.

But after? An order based on the balance of powers has become unworkable, primarily because powers no longer oppose each other face to face but on many sides. And nor do they accept the principle of dividing up areas of influence. The Islamic world has never been willing to reason in such terms. Ali Khamenei, successor of Khomeini, translated Sayyid Qutb's *The Future of This Religion* and in his introduction he wrote that "this lofty and great author" had confirmed in his book how "world government shall be in the hands of our school and 'the future belongs to Islam.'" That was in 1967—and it was valid for Sunnites and Shiites alike. Tenacious and farsighted plans.

But it wasn't this that convinced Kissinger about the impracticability of a world order, however necessary and however "desperately" it is being pursued. It was the fact that there is no longer a circumscribed and roughly regulated space in which politics is being carried out. Having quoted General Keith Alexander, the commander of American Cyber Command, according to whom "the next war will begin in cyberspace," Kissinger immediately commented: "It will not be possible to conceive of international order when the region through which states' survival and progress are taking place remains without any international standards of conduct and is left to unilateral decisions." A definition in which Kissinger is forced to mix the language of Westphalia with the language of cyberspace, leaving the impression that the latter eludes not only the former, but eludes political leaders themselves.

The recurring obsession throughout the twentieth century was that of *social control*. Once society had become a sovereign entity, free from all restrictions, it could control and shape its own matter. The various totalitarian forms were each an attempt in this direction. But the states themselves were operational in appearance only. Installed within each state was a smaller structure that was attached to it but could also maneuver it. This is what happened with the KGB in the USSR, and with the SS in Germany. They were sectarian bodies that held unlimited powers. They had many methods of control, traceable to two main rules that Orwell observed in Oceania: "Who controls the past controls the future: who controls the present controls the past."

But this wouldn't be the final method of control. When the digital empire was established at the beginning of the new millennium it became clear that *control* meant firstly *control of data*. And the situation was reversed. Data was no longer extracted by force from above, but was spontaneously offered from below, by countless individuals. And it was the very material over which to exercise control. The question then arose: what would be the controlling power? The first suspects, as always, were states. But a startling novelty was introduced. States were not the only ones who could act. Starting with them, there is a sequence that includes above all the businesses where data is constantly flowing—and extends as far as IT gangs (of criminals? of activists furthering some good cause?) and the anonymous, lone hacker, who could just even be playing with his power. Anonymity is the crucial point.

In this way there is a kind of return to the beginning: every society freed from religious commitments is at first an anonymous entity. Then it identifies with certain forms of state, rooted in certain places. Then with sects within those states. Finally with giant businesses that collect and control data. But the sequence doesn't end there. We then get into an area *that has no name*. And where names can no longer be attributed with any certainty. Just as in the beginning. It is irrelevant whether a certain power over data is used to govern or disrupt the evolution of an order, since control is measured only on the effectiveness of the action. If the order itself is judged to be evil, the virus that neutralizes it becomes the weapon wielded by the forces of good. And could just as well be wielded by an anonymous name or entity.

The Italian translation for the word *hacker, pirata informatico* (IT pirate), is inaccurate and misleading, since it ignores the *action on the form* which is inherent in the English term. A hacker is someone who cuts, damages, and—if necessary—dismantles, reassembles, smashes a form. Without this action on form there is no *hacking*, whereas piracy is a simple act of attack and appropriation. Interference with software, manipulation, derailment: these are features that recall Dada and pervade the cloud like uncontrollable storms. All software requires coding operations. And the world is being subjected to a procedure of universal and

coding

omnilateral coding. All coding is a substitution. But coding can also be substituted, even by a "malicious code," as it is generally termed in computer jargon. This is the *karman* of digitality. He who causes harm by substitution can easily perish by substitution.

Legitimacy finally vanished when the German chancellor Theobald von Bethmann-Hollweg declared that treaties weren't worth the paper they were written on, and World War I began. But remnants of legitimacy remained in the language of politics, just as certain families continually recount stories about aristocratic ancestors. And the word is always used with a certain complacency.

For those countries, however, who have never had the privilege of democracy and occupy a large part of the world, legitimacy entails primarily, if not exclusively, obeying the outcome of elections. But if the West undermines election results in these countries, as happened in Algeria and in Egypt, all its well-intentioned sermonizing in favor of democracy will be seen as a mockery and as confirmation of the old, widely held notion that it is wise to think twice before following what the West seeks to promote.

Democracy's open wound is the possibility of someone reaching power by legitimate means, but with the aim of abolishing democracy itself, as happened with Hitler in January 1933. It is an untreatable and noble wound, since it demonstrates that democracy is like a living being that harbors within it the seed of self-destruction. Whenever there is any attempt to heal the wound with drastic treatment, generally by armed revolt, it opens a path that eventually leads the way to future disasters. In Algeria, in 1991, the Islamic party (ISF, Islamic Salvation Front, an eloquent name) had won a clear victory in the elections. According to the rules of democracy, the Islamic party ought to have assumed power, and it had enough seats to change the constitution and transform the country from a secular to a religious state. What followed was a military coup, unanimously supported by Western powers. The result was a civil war in which some 150,000 were killed. A large proportion had their throats slit. Another civil war in the 1990s, in Yugoslavia, would lead to a similar number of dead. But the cruel, relentless sequence of events there is still remembered today. So far as the civil war in Algeria there has been an almost unbroken silence. And yet it was on that occasion that a Salafi group, the GSPC (Groupe Salafiste pour la Prédication et le Combat), precursor of al-Qaeda and of ISIS, took their first tentative steps. Their action was based on a renewed, total, and in this case reasoned mistrust of the West. It showed that Islamic fundamentalism had no prejudices about its adversaries: it could attack Westerners or other Muslims, Sunni or Shia, with just as much zeal.

Secular thought is prouder of nothing more than having invented democracy. With good reason, since no other political form could provide a tolerable living standard for such a large number of people. But democracy, more than the idea of *something*, is a concatenation of procedures. Procedures that function best when their wheels are well oiled in accordance with the model of *formal* democracy. An admirable and fragile model, which can operate only in specific conditions. The prime enemy of democracy is demography, which makes it impracticable as soon as certain population thresholds are exceeded. But if democracy is unable to provide effective guarantees (tolerance, freedom of expression, equal rights, cosmopolitanism, nonviolent transfer of power), it becomes increasingly difficult to use such guarantees as principles that uphold the idea. Democracy then becomes more and more a *wishful nothing*. And, in memory, it takes on the hue of a lost stage set. People will one day talk about it in the same way as when the Imperial senators harked back to the virtues of ancient Rome.

Whenever the formal nature of democracy is mentioned, many show signs of impatience and are quick to say that democracy is never sufficiently democratic, and to be true democracy it ought to be substantial, and that one day perhaps it will be, and democracy will then be quite another thing . . . At which point we can be quite certain that the person speaking is an enemy of democracy.

After all, what united Lenin and Hitler in the first place was an aversion to formal democracy. Everything else followed as a consequence, in divergent, though not so distant, directions. The wonder of democracy lies in its being empty, with no content. It is a doctrine for which regulation is essential, even before that which the regulation prescribes. And the risk is that this essential characteristic of democracy may be considered too abstract to stir respect and admiration.

Formal democracy is without doubt the most perfect version of democracy, but also the least applicable. Especially when a certain meridian of history has been overstepped and demographic, ethnic, psychic pressures become overwhelming. Then the chimera of direct democracy looms again. It is founded on a hatred of mediation, which easily becomes a hatred of thought itself, which is part and parcel of mediation. All the more precious are—and will be—those remaining rocks of formal democracy, battered and often submerged by the waves of something that proves more or less disastrous.

Only in the American Declaration of Independence is "the pursuit of Happiness" described as one of the "inalienable rights" of man—and this is often remembered as a benefit bestowed by the Founding Fathers compared to the more arid European constitutions. But that magical word is also used in another text, which can be regarded as the terrorist Declaration of Independence: the *Catechism of a Revolutionary*, drawn up by Sergey Nechayev. Article 22 reads: "The Society has no aim other than the complete liberation and happiness of the masses."

"The greatest happiness for the greatest number": at first sight, it seems an expression of generic democratic benevolence. If examined more closely, it seems laden with unexpected consequences. Outlined by Francis Hutcheson and Claude Adrien Helvétius, used again by Joseph Priestley and Cesare Beccaria ("the greatest happiness divided into the greatest number"), the formula emerged a few years later in Jeremy Bentham, revealing with him its malevolent aspect. Bentham was searching among human feelings and impulses for something that could be measured. He found it in utility. But that was not enough. *Everything* had to be measured. And Bentham discovered that it could be, if related to utility. As for utility itself, it could be measured in money. At this point, thought Bentham, people could start reasoning in a valid, scientific way.

It was a fateful moment that went unnoticed by all except Bentham's faithful followers. It was the pretext for political economy, then in its initial stage of grand and turbulent expansion, to take over the whole of humanity, feeding all of its components into its calculations, like market commodities. It didn't matter that these were entities perhaps not measurable at all—or at least measured using primitive and arbitrary criteria. What mattered was that everything could now be measured. Economics—no longer just called political economy—would soon become the supreme discipline on which everything else depended, and its countless representatives, up to the algorithmicians of today, would practice it. They may often not have heard of Bentham, but were putting his principles into practice—principles that rested on a false foundation, yet were easy to apply. And economics, like the world that came to be governed by it, was particularly eager to apply itself. To everything.

What, asked Tocqueville, is the ultimate purpose of democracy? And what irrevocably distinguishes it from aristocracy? First of all, the wish to experiment: "Among aristocratic peoples, social power usually limited itself to directing and to overseeing citizens in everything that had a direct and visible connection to the national interest; it willingly abandoned them to their free will in everything else." The attitude of democratic governors was quite another: "You would say that they consider themselves responsible for the actions and for the individual destiny of their subjects, that they have undertaken to lead and to enlighten each one of them in the different acts of his life, and as needed, to make him happy despite himself."

Without expressing his own opinion, and always maintaining a false semblance of neutrality, Tocqueville had introduced a crucial argument *against* democracy. Why accept a regime that wants to make us happy "despite ourselves"? Just as one day it compelled someone to be happy, so the next day that regime could compel the same person to transform himself into something even more unpleasant than enforced happiness.

> There is nothing more formless than the substance
> of minds, if one separates it from God.
>
> MALEBRANCHE

The figure of *Homo saecularis* didn't have to wait for the emergence of paleoanthropologists, nor for the countless conferences on secularization: he had already been described in the twelfth century by a Benedictine monk, Peter of Celle: "From the window of quiet and contemplation, let us survey how the voluble wheel of secular life rolls around and then we shall be able to grasp the great inconstancy with which secular conscience (*saecularis conscientia*) spins around. Just as wandering, worldly care knows no stable foundation, so secular conscience furnishes no sure and stable signs of itself. It changes its expressions not just from day to day and year to year, but hour by hour and practically every moment. Look at the forum, the tavern, the theatre, the brothel: they are all workshops of error. Secular man (*homo saecularis*) is here, there, everywhere."

Homo saecularis was evidently already accompanying history like a perpetual shadow. What has been added to this picture of him, with the passing of the centuries? The fact that the shadow has been transformed into *normal man*, who finds himself a solitary, hapless protagonist at the center of the stage.

Unlike Vedic man, who was born with the burden of four *ṛṇas*, "debts"—to the gods, to the *ṛṣis*, to ancestors, and to mankind in general—*Homo saecularis* owes nothing to anyone. He stands by himself. He has nothing *behind*, apart from what he himself does. There is an inevitable sense of uncertainty, since he rests on something unstable—and perhaps insubstantial. The pleasure of arbitrary will is marred by that lack of substance. Arbitrary will, but up to what point? There is no model to emulate, not even for pleasure. There is sovereignty—prior to an object over which to exercise it. This is the perennial worry of *Homo saecularis*, who is nonetheless reluctant to talk about it.

Every religion demands an observance of precepts. These, varying in time and place, can also be onerous, obsessive, exasperating. Or they can be reduced to a minimum, which remains nevertheless mandatory. *Homo saecularis* however is not bound to follow precepts. He must simply avoid breaching various regulations on which his life is based. But he is not obliged to perform any action.

Homo saecularis can, strictly speaking, live his life unnoticed and undisturbed, playing no part in what is going on around him. Literature has left us various examples of such lives (Dostoyevsky's Underground Man, Bartleby, the voices in Robert Walser's monologues). Apart from certain elementary rules, which persuade people not to disturb their neighbors so as not to be disturbed by them, it became possible to live a life free of restraints, pleasant or contemptible *in itself*, in the absence of doctrinal precepts. But this has not in fact happened. Even if precepts no longer depend on a particular religion, they have promptly returned to fill the head of *Homo saecularis*, creating alternate feelings of puzzlement, confusion, transient enthusiasm, or deep depression.

Secularization means, in the first place, a slackening of obligations—of any obligation. And, in certain cases, an elimination of such obligations. Apart from respecting laws, which implies the observance of an order, the only obligation that remains in every circumstance is the payment of taxes. No ritual is compulsory, not even that of voting. The resulting situation may rouse a subtle sense of euphoria. There, before the eyes of all, is a vast arena of what is available. And of what is permissible, so long as it is lawful.

But the secularists are not happy. Nor do they feel relieved of great burdens. They feel the insubstantiality of all that surrounds them. At times they recognize something ominous in it. But in what respect? The same insubstantiality exists in they themselves. *Personalized.*

Secularization was perhaps already taking place in the Upper Paleolithic age—and the process has continued uninterrupted. But when can it be said that secularity finally took over? During the years when Adorno was writing *Minima moralia*, therefore around 1950 in the United States. The word *secularity* was not in current usage and no one thought of celebrating its arrival. It was then that the world of detached houses with small fenced gardens, an improbable world until that time, became *normality.* And normality replaced the norm. All of this might have been welcomed with relief, as if people were escaping from a series of constraints. But this was not how it was. Indeed, a muted rancor, with no apparent objective, very soon began to develop. When an international youth movement began to protest in the campuses and lecture halls against the *system*, that rancor was already beginning to be voiced, even if its targets could be illusory and misleading.

Secularity doesn't seek to convince. It seeks only to be applied. After all, it consists of no more than a series of procedures. And these procedures want only to be considered as equivalent to normality. If we have to fly from one place to another, a series of steps have to be performed: those and no others. In the same way that air traffic obeys a certain number of regulations that are applied everywhere. That is normality. But the same happens with the financialization of the economy. And with IT everywhere, the uncontested realm of procedures is established. Once this is accepted, much follows from it. Every other view of the course of things becomes like a guest who is welcome only if he respects ongoing procedures.

All of this follows from a time in history when procedures have taken command over rituals. A moment that is elusive, hard to establish, since the two powers also have features in common. First of all, they are both formalized actions. But they aim in opposite directions. Ritual aims toward perfect awareness, which for Catholics is the moment of transubstantiation. Procedures, on the other hand, point toward total automatism. The more procedures multiply, the more the realm of automata expands.

And the moment came when secularists rebelled. They realized they were not alone. And that they didn't occupy the entire world. Procedures were applied everywhere, but the secularists were living only in a certain part of the planet—and not even in the *major* part. They suddenly felt under siege from *foreigners*, whom they called *migrants*. Who wanted to use their procedures, but continued to watch them with the untrustworthy eye of those who do not feel at home. To see them strolling about in familiar streets already instilled a feeling of unease. After so much past suffering and deprivation, did they now have to hand over all they had achieved to those malevolent—and, above all, so numerous—beings?

Secular society has a tremendous fear of what has been its greatest discovery: relief and release from ritual and confessional obligations. Instead of appreciating this state of suspension and treating it as a possible beginning for new ways forward, people become caught up in *causes*, whether good or bad, as Max Stirner had seen. And those *causes* are first of all palliative.

But where can that which doesn't renounce thought be accommodated? No longer in the university. Thought would benefit more than ever from a period of concealment, of a covert and clandestine existence, from which to reemerge in a situation that might resemble that of the Pre-Socratics. The powers have to be *recognized* before even naming them and venturing to theorize the world. Nietzsche's "impure thought" took the first steps in this direction. But the world cannot be said to have gone much further.

The era of religions ended with Islam. Muhammad emerged as "Seal of the Prophets." From then on, only schisms are born. Or sects and cults, which multiply. Meanwhile, the worm of secularization, present from the very beginning, is ever more apparent and corrosive in its operation. More or less hidden, it was already recognizable in every cosmogony. But what happens when the religious sap no longer flows? Secular thought reigns. Yet it is insufficient, inadequate even in relation to the elementary facts of life. In the long run, secularists develop a resentment—sometimes even violent—of secularity itself. There is then a renewed attraction toward the sects: they at least offer solid support. Or toward crude principles and awkward measures for self-defense. The secular world, abandoned to itself, offers not security but probabilities. Science is a world apart, inhabited by few. And it hasn't developed rigorous rules of conduct, other than a general attitude of trust in science itself. As soon as scientists leave their laboratories, which may only be laboratories of the mind, they find themselves in the same situation as other secular beings, and often talk like hapless individuals. What holds everything together is the operation of prostheses. Ceaseless, far more powerful than any human action, that operation is the background noise for every thought. Which is evidence that prostheses as a whole are moving ahead and protect their propagators like innocuous and often irrelevant guests.

Is there such a thing as *secular thought*? Or is it a convenient figment? Or is it a ragbag of other thoughts? Disconcerting though it seems, one has to admit it really does exist. Its ingenuous and ruthless prophet was Bentham. His shrine is University College London, where his mummy is on display. And his last missionary was B. F. Skinner, founder of behaviorism, whom the scientific community accepted without objection for some while. The subject of Skinner's experiments was the perfect *Homo saecularis*, who exists only as the sum of *reinforced* reactions. Skinner's man, considered today as an incongruous remnant of the past, was a diligent experimental application of Locke's *tabula rasa*. And Locke was the first gentleman to assume the role of *Homo saecularis*.

Secular thought is what remains after a gradual process of emptying away, operating over several millennia. Animals, gods (in the plural or the singular), demons, angels, saints, souls, spirits, and lastly also principles and will, have been gradually removed. And have become materials for research. All still present, but in books. Meanwhile, everyday thought has been increasingly willing to dispense with books themselves.

Homo saecularis speaks with many, often divergent, voices. The most conspicuous of these voices is progressive and humanitarian. It applies precepts inherited from Christianity, softened and sweetened. A timid and faint solution, it corresponds, in the reverse sense, with the move taking place in the Church itself, which is trying more and more to resemble a welfare institution. The result is that secularists speak with priestly compunction and priests try to pass themselves off as professors of sociology.

Quite different was the tone of more consistent and rigorous secularists, such as the early nineteenth-century English radicals. These are well exemplified by John Stuart Mill, who could describe himself with admirable frankness: "I am one of the very few examples, in this country, of one who has, not thrown off religious belief, but never had it: I grew up in a negative state with regard to it." A very understandable situation if we look at the education he had received from his father, who had not only begun to teach him Greek at the age of three, so that he had read the whole of Herodotus by eight, but had instilled in him several principles that he felt should belong to every *Homo saecularis*: "I have a hundred times heard him say, that all ages and nations have represented their gods as wicked, in a constantly increasing progression, that mankind have gone on adding trait after trait till they reached the most perfect conception of wickedness which the human mind can devise, and have called this God, and prostrated themselves before it. This *ne plus ultra* of wickedness he considered to be embodied in what is commonly presented to mankind as the creed of Christianity." This is how *Homo saecularis* spoke in his original and unadulterated state.

Christian theologians have been trying for centuries to answer the most serious question: *Si Deus est, unde malum?* If God exists, where does evil come from? And all the answers, over time, were regarded by someone or other as inadequate. But there is also another, no less serious, question that Leibniz formulated along exactly the same lines: "*Si [Deus] non est, unde bonum?*" If [God] does not exist, where does goodness come from? The origins of evil and of goodness are equally obscure. But those who tried to answer the first question, from Saint Augustine to Leibniz himself, were often supreme metaphysicians; whereas answers to the second have so far been primitive, coming from the garrulous promoters of a lay morality—led by Flaubert's Monsieur Homais—or from Neo-Darwinian scientists eager to marry evolution with fine sentiments.

Secularism is defined in negative terms, in that it ignores and excludes the divine, the sacred, the gods or the one god. Once this part has been taken away, everything

43

can be included in secularism. But there is one eminent form of it, which stands out and is clearly distinguishable from every other. It is *humanist secularism*, a way of thought that adheres to its own principles no less than the religions that have gone before it. And places its faith no longer in transcendent beings but in a body described as *humanity*. Toward which—according to Charles Taylor, who dedicated a thousand pages to it in *A Secular Age*—it has a duty to promote "prosperity." This term, however, only has an unambiguous meaning in relation to gross domestic product. It is easy to imagine how Dostoyevsky's Underground Man would sneer if asked what human "prosperity" is. Otherwise, the question of what the world is, what it is made of, ought to be one for science. But science is continually offering new answers to it. What, then, remains fixed and sacrosanct? A certain number of rules: the dominance of fine feelings, definable as various forms of altruism; tolerance toward ideas and forms of behavior, within the broadest possible limits; respect for the wishes of the majority and certain essential procedural notions of democracy, such as the separation of powers. All of this together creates something that can only be described as a form of religion, if by this we mean—following Lactantius and Tertullian—an indissoluble *bond* between certain principles and forms of behavior. Humanist secularism is therefore described not as something that comes *after* religions and *against* religions, but as a form of religion itself, which has only recently become worldwide. This new entity is able to accommodate within it all the various existing religions and sects, in the same way that Imperial Rome accommodated the cult of Isis or Mithras or the Syriac Jews. Yet keeping a capacity to react with force against certain forms considered unacceptable, like Christianity in its early centuries, or Islamic fundamentalism today. In its appearance, humanist secularism (otherwise called *laïcité* in France) includes every shade of expression found in previous religions, from lukewarm allegiance to aggressive zeal.

laïcité

Homo saecularis is a sophisticated and complex product of evolution and history. But this doesn't mean he understands who he is, nor what the world in front of him is. In any event, what the Knight of Malta Sacramozo asks in Hofmannsthal's *Andreas* is just as true for him: "I beg you to treat my soul carefully." If only because *Homo saecularis* is made of time and metamorphosis. His most appealing aspect is sheer potentiality, much greater than that of his ancestors. Now he could move in a very great number of different directions. But this doesn't mean he is aware of them. He might as well remain a good unaware man. And he might easily be accused of being responsible for every kind of misdemeanor. But, in his defense, it is right to consider what the Western world would be if it were governed by its most implacable internal dissidents, by those who preach *radical emancipation*—whatever that may be—and who set about *reinventing communism*. Imposture thrives, in the land of gullible people.

Two thousand years after Christ, secularism envelops the planet. This is not because it has conquered religions but because it is the first, of all religions, to turn not to external entities but to itself, as a just and ultimate vision of things as they are, and as they have to be.

If the twentieth century was the century of reflexivity, this character is also apparent in the fact that society regards itself as something that now incorporates everything, thanks to that invincible weapon that goes under the name of technology.

With secularization, the meaning of religion tends to fade. And religions themselves, when they don't die out, tend to splinter into parties, large and small. After all, it's only a question of opinions, which could coexist and alternately predominate, without conflict. But opinions can harden and become entrenched. They morph into dangerous weapons. Then all can end again in civil war—an updated form of the religious war.

The word *humanist*, taken out of the context in which it first emerged—the fifteenth-century Florence of Poggio Bracciolini and Coluccio Salutati, of Marsilio Ficino and Pico della Mirandola—sounds shrill and pompous. It is the first word anyone turns to when they want to impose a benevolent but coercive agenda. Charles Taylor attached to it the adjective *self-sufficient*, but it was a superfluous addition. Or useful only for thwarting any investigation into the assumptions behind that form of humanism. An inquiry that would soon get tripped up by vague generalities. Though they will hate to hear such words, there is no way of avoiding it: secularists are pious folk. And secular humanists could be their priests.

Particularly odd is the claim that secular humanists are

most proud of: that they have rid themselves of all faith. To act for the good of a Church or to act for the good of a society; to act in sight of divine good or the good of humanity: these are radically different acts, but are joined together by the existence of a *faith*. And, if that is enough to make them religious acts, then all are to be equally regarded as such.

The eighteenth-century forebears of today's secularists would often say that everything had to be traced back to matter if plausible explanations were to be found. But this operation has become increasingly baffling and impracticable, since scientists are no longer prepared to say what matter itself is. Having disposed of matter, which proved to be an expanse of quicksand, people tried (and are still stubbornly trying) to rely upon another unshakable *primum*: evolution.

From evolution there have been countless attempts to derive the necessity and justness of fine feelings—and above all of altruism. The good of evolution became the good of a single species, but this terminological slip did not, according to some, affect the scientific validity of the theories. Which yet had great difficulty in being articulated. Not least because the theory of evolution served, over the years— with equal readiness and equal lack of evidence—as a basis for the most brutal or most well-meaning extrapolations. Even the principles of eugenics, zealously applied in civilized Scandinavian countries as well as Hitler's Germany, made reference to Darwin's theories. The plan to establish a humanitarian ethic based on evolution remained, like every other attempt at founding a lay morality, at the stage of *wishful thinking*. It is—Baudelaire noted in Belgium—a funeral carriage perpetually followed by the "multitude of free thinkers."

But pure secularists, lacking any religious affiliation and not much inclined toward spiritualistic fancies, cannot do without the *need to feel good*. Their ideal would be for some Neo-Darwinian biologist to demonstrate that society has been based, from the very beginning, on altruism and tolerance. And therefore, that being good constitutes an *evolutionary advantage*, the only criterion with which they can measure good. Every year, someone eagerly attempts to demonstrate it, in vain.

The secular world is ready to follow all sorts of theories, especially those that claim to be scientifically based. But there are also revelations that it isn't able to deal with because it finds them difficult to recognize. Simone Weil had that ability, and she exercised it without letting herself be intimidated by history: "The Gospel is the last and marvelous expression of Greek genius, just as the *Iliad* is its first." To arrive at assertions like this, it was assumed that Greece and the Gospels were two independent and non-discordant revelations. To show how that recognition was reached, Weil used the metaphor of looking at a cubic box: "There is no viewpoint from which the box has the appearance of a cube: one always sees only a few sides, the corners do not seem right angles, the sides do not seem equal. No one has ever seen, no one will ever see a cube.

For like reasons, no one has ever touched nor will ever touch a cube. If one moves around the box, an infinite variety of apparent forms is generated. None of these is the cubic form." At the same time we well know that the cubic form constitutes the unity of all those changeable forms. And "also their truth," added Weil, who considered this to be a divine gift, so that "enclosed in our very sensibility is a revelation." From this revelation one could move on to understand all the others. So that the *Iliad* could be a revelation to which the Gospel was linked—or the *Bhagavad Gītā*. This would seem obvious. But for the secular world the cubic box *does not exist*.

Homo saecularis is not so opposed to religions as such. Religions are very similar to ideologies—and he comes across ideologies every day. Those who say they are Christian cannot differ very much from those who say they are vegetarian. They are all groups, communities, confraternities. People can be Communists—as well as bodybuilders. Each choice has to be respected. They are all minorities. Niches. But what *Homo saecularis* cannot understand is the divine. He doesn't know where to place it. It doesn't fit into the order of things. Of his things.

Divine and *sacred*: what happens when someone who is not inclined to profess any religion recognizes those two words and his experience of them is no less intense than that of a religious believer? He will have to admit that those two words indicate something that exists in itself, even before and beyond any creed. And this itself is an invitation to pierce the protective and suffocating shell that is the superstition of society.

The divine is what *Homo saecularis* has carefully, persistently erased. He has even deleted it from the lexicon of *that which is*. But the divine is not like a rock, which everyone inevitably sees. The divine needs to be recognized. And recognition is the supreme act toward the divine. A sporadic, momentary act that cannot be transposed into a state. *"Incessu patuit dea,"* the divine is like the footstep of a goddess, who moves ahead and suddenly goes further. The divine is a discontinuous flicker, which relates to something complete and continuous. For *Homo saecularis* all this was indistinct and contrary to the physiology he had developed in himself. It was vain, then, to point his own desires in that direction. Of all the varieties of *Homo saecularis* only the members of the Society of the Friends of Crime, as recounted by Sade, knew how to put into action precise, detailed, unambiguous desires.

John Stuart Mill recounted how, "From the winter of 1821, when I first read Bentham, and especially from the commencement of the Westminster Review, I had what might truly be called an object in life; to be a reformer of the world. My conception of my own happiness was entirely identified with this object. [. . .] I was accustomed to felicitate myself on the certainty of a happy life which I enjoyed, through placing my happiness in something durable and distant, in which some progress might be always making, while it could never be exhausted by complete attainment." And so it was, for five years, "during which the general improvement going on in the world and the idea of myself as engaged with others in struggling to promote it, seemed enough to fill up an interesting and animated existence." Until one day, Mill continued, "I awakened from this as from a dream." What had happened? He found himself pondering a question: "Suppose that all your objects in life were realized; that all the changes in institutions and opinions which you are looking forward to, could be completely effected at this very instant: would this be a great joy and happiness to you?" Mill was saddened to realize that the answer was a distinct "No!" He felt his heart sink: "The whole foundation on which my life was constructed fell down." Everything was suddenly "insipid or indifferent." Months of deep depression followed, which lasted through the winter of 1826–1827. Outwardly nothing had changed. Mill continued his very active life: "During this period I was not incapable of my usual occupations. [. . .] I had been so drilled in a certain sort of mental exercise, that I could still carry it on when all the spirit had gone out of it. I even composed and spoke several speeches at the debating society, how, or with what degree of success, I know not."

Mill is still regarded today as one of the luminaries of liberalism. But liberals of every kind, whether lay or religious, never had the capacity and bold clear-sightedness to ask the question that Mill, with spotless probity, asked of himself—and it made him fall into a state that only Coleridge could describe: "A grief without a pang, void, dark, and drear."

The whole secular and democratic world is founded on free will and on the belief in science. But science shows no sign of belief in the existence of free will. Indeed, on the basis of various arguments and experiments, it rejects it. Meanwhile, public life goes on as though this were not the case. Otherwise judicial, administrative, political, and economic systems would immediately grind to a halt. The dilemma is so serious that it is not recognized.

From Benjamin Libet to Daniel Wegner and Chun Siong Soon, the experiments usually referred to in order to support the rejection of free will relate to *decisions*, such as whether or not to press a certain button. But the moment of *motor* decision is only a tiny part of the conscious continuum. What happens in a state of immobility, such as when someone is sitting in an armchair awake, or contemplating, or reading a book? Science can offer only two types of answer: neurons that shoot electric charges, or subatomic events. But how can we establish that these events occur a few milliseconds before their conscious counterpart if we don't know what that counterpart consists of? And in any event, how could we interpret those neural events in terms of consciousness? Through what intermediaries? Each time it would be a route on which the starting point can be defined with great precision, whereas the end point would remain invariably uncertain.

At a meeting of top-level academics it is taken for granted that no religious believers will be there but that everyone aims to be decent. No one will belong to a religious creed (apart from exceptions that fall within the sphere of eccentricity) but everyone shares certain basic principles of behavior and judgment. However, a chasm opens up when anyone begins to investigate what those points of agreement are founded on. And no other social group appeals so often to freedom (of research, of thought), while at the same time firmly rejecting free will.

Absorbed in thought, they gather more and more often to discuss the vicissitudes of religions: are they on the way to extinction? Can they—at last—be regarded as museum pieces? Can they be shelved away in some university archive? Or do they show some sign of new life, of perhaps returning, in some fervid revival? And how can such persistence and resistance be explained? Opinions conflict and converge, canceling one another out. In common they have only a scarce inclination to deal with the substance of the religions themselves. The prevailing idea is that they should be seen as a social phenomenon along with many others, and therefore to be studied for their influence on collective behaviors. What they actually claim to be seems of secondary importance. Meanwhile there is a constant growth of something else: gullibility.

There is an inescapable dividing line between secularism and religion, drawn by ritual. Secularists cannot accept the performance of acts toward an external entity at regular and sometimes fixed moments of time. Acts that demand an invisible witness. For secularists, that invisible witness simply doesn't exist. And the word *ritual* itself is associated with something ornamental, tedious, ineffectual. Therefore the exact opposite of what the word used to mean in other civilizations.

This repudiation of ritual—or at least its relegation to the margins of existence—could have resulted in a joyous reprieve from acts of obligation. But this hasn't happened. Tacitly, though firmly, the secular brain has resigned itself to thinking that it cannot do without repeated and rigidly formalized acts, not only where it is recognized as having some effectiveness, for example in the sphere of justice, but in every aspect of existence, even in its most fatuous and most private areas. Banished rituality has in the end reentered society, seeping into its remotest veins. Secular life is increasingly interspersed with situations that must involve behaving *in a certain way*, like moving from one television format to another. Prescribed rules and fashions have spread everywhere—and tend to become more subtle and differentiated. But nothing in them is directed at anything external to society itself. Each time they are tautological assertions that emphasize what is existent, in the same way that certain ancient rituals emphasized reverence for the divinity.

For some of the great corporations, such as Google, the substance that is turned into money and feeds it is no longer petroleum but advertising. Its impressive economic relevance, which is the exoteric face of advertising, must not however deter us from contemplating its esoteric aspect, which is repetition. It is essential that advertising is repeated, in the same way as ritual acts. Repetition assures constancy of meaning. And this is the very task that society has delegated to advertising. This is no small matter, indeed it is a function that establishes the meaning of every single act. The esoteric aim of advertising is therefore an endless expansion and reiteration of images and brands that become wedged in every cavity of the mind. And if they were not there keeping watch, everything might seem colorless and shapeless. Instead, it is a nonstop celebration, from which there is no escape. A process that culminates and is sanctioned by social media, where spontaneous self-exhibition goes together with compulsory publicity. As if whatever appears could in no way be separated from advertising.

I remember an Italian TV variety show in which one of the contestants was an ordinary young girl from a remote Italian province. She was plump, pretty, vacuous. The program format required the presenter to ask three girls a few questions. It was now the turn of the plump contestant. "What would you like to be?" asked the presenter. "Advertising," replied the girl. The presenter remained impassive. "And why?" she asked. "Because everyone sees it," said the girl. It was followed by a ritual burst of applause from the hidden audience. Thus spoke the *Zeitgeist*.

If secularists are faithful to their beliefs and yet follow some form of ritual, however fragmented or idiosyncratic, then what separates secularists from religious believers? Only a certain quality of perception. In comparison with religious believers, secularists are like what tourists are to natives. Curious, sympathetic, sometimes enthusiastic, often impressed. And they, the tourists, are always buoyed up by one comforting thought: their return to the place they came from. In relation to natives, tourists are open-minded and flexible. As well as ready to move on, without more ado, to visit *other* natives, even farther afield. But what they see is never *the thing* that natives see, which could be (who can say?) the *ultimate thing*—provided, at least, that by *natives* we don't mean those debasing and prearranged scenes put on for the benefit of foreign visitors, since natives are now almost only to be found in books or in places where they are constrained to celebrate rituals for extreme tourists. One other possibility remains: to travel back in time, perhaps toward remote entities, accessible only through surviving texts. Perhaps also to mingle with a Vedic caravan. And at that time tourists did not exist.

Homo saecularis is inevitably a tourist. Not just when he is traveling. Channel and web surfing form a vast part of his mental activity. They are operations that already existed, which one day took on the shape that these terms indicated. Bouvard and Pécuchet already practiced them without any technological devices.

If he is not traveling on business, if he is not a migrant, *Homo saecularis* can only be classified, at each border crossing, as a tourist. And this disturbs him. He enjoys watching tourists, and even bemoaning them. He wouldn't want to be confused with them. This embarrassment reveals, in *Homo saecularis*, a dark presentiment about his own insubstantiality. If not a tourist, what else could he be? And "tourist" is a category that is supranational, worldwide, undifferentiated, as indeed *Homo saecularis* generally is. But that definition then implies a community too large, which swamps every distinctive detail. Whereas for *Homo saecularis*, his last refuge is to feel he is something special.

In the first of the modern ages—during the time of Alexander the Great—"cosmopolitans" began to appear, so called because they behaved like traders, moving from one place to another and from one tribe to another without any essential change in their way of being, but adapting to local customs, according to circumstances. Some stood in their way and looked on them with suspicion because of their readiness to coexist with tribes of very different sorts. In certain times and places they kept a low profile. They were not welcome. But more recently, first in Europe and then in the Americas, they reemerged under the name of "tourists." And, almost to their own surprise, they realized they were spreading everywhere. They were a slow, relentless tide, a tribe that tended to absorb all tribes within it. They were not attached to one territory and easily found themselves in faraway continents. They communicated among one another first of all because they used the same procedures. In other respects, their ideas could not be very different either. They were all tourists.

Hidden among secularists, and always few in number, are *analogists*. These people consider other secularists as divided into sects with which they are familiar but feel no attraction. There have always been *analogists*. They sought the *signaturae rerum*, and also encountered them while moving from one continent to another. They were the first not to pay close attention to tribal prohibitions, whose significances they nevertheless recognized and had sometimes elaborated. The Vedic seers, the *ṛṣis*, they called "gymnosophists," "naked wise men," and they knew that their ideas converged. They were the first to understand that thought did not depend on society, but society on thought. This made them suspicious. Their detractors referred to the *fœtor gnosticus*. They were to be found among Christians as among pagans, among Jews as among Arabs, among Iranians as among Indians. They were never numerous, but were recognizable. Even if they would often disguise themselves. Sometimes they had access to the *arcana imperii*, indeed sometimes they held the reins of power. Sometimes they were excluded from it, like the most treacherous enemies. They liked to contemplate, more than act. But, for some, the grid of certain actions, even political actions, became an object of contemplation. This is what happened, for example, with Leibniz. They did not preach, they did not convert. They talked and they wrote. They relied on the simple power of the word, on their ability to turn people's hearts toward a new East. It was impossible to disappoint them, for they expected nothing from the world. Their only satisfaction was their investigation, which was never-ending. René Daumal was a shining example of an analogist and was well aware of it. His life's work, necessarily unfinished, was *Mount Analogue*.

Until recently, when American citizens were required to state their religious affiliation on an official document, in the case of secularists there were two possible ways out: to declare themselves *atheist* or *agnostic*. But there is always something drastic and final about saying "atheist," whereas "agnostic" is inevitably bland and vague. There was much dissatisfaction about both definitions. And so an acronym came into being (since an acronym alone is now a guarantee of existence): SBNR—Spiritual But Not Religious. Estimations of the number in this group vary, but it is substantial. And a whole literature has emerged to document this. People talk about SBNR rather like LGBT. It's another way of creating an identity: a word that is the Arabian Phoenix for the new millennium.

But who are these SBNRs? Obviously they are secularists who feel they don't fit into any available categories. Intolerant of all religion, to the point of rejecting it in their acronym—a curious fact, since acronyms by their nature are affirmative—SBNRs are yet inclined to dilute some part of the "religious" substance into another category— "spiritual"—whose confines are very vague. Those who gaze at a glorious sunset and think there is *something* more in what they see are already heading full sail into the "spiritual." And they will move around there as passionate tourists, even if they don't reach the condition of "passionate pilgrim," for they avoid every sanctuary.

Since the acronym SBNR contains an adversative and a negation, it is easy to infer that its adherents intend to

stand firmly opposed to something. Which is the last letter: R for "religious." In no circumstances, it seems, do they
want to be considered "religious." But to be "spiritual" requires some reliance on a *spirit*. For Christians, the spirit is
one of the three persons of the Trinity; for Jews, "the spirit
of Elohim glided over the waters" from the first day; for
Muslims, everything comes from a line of the Koran,
where the prophet says: "The Spirit is the command of my
Lord." But what thing are secularists (who include SBNRs,
like a new sect) referring to when they talk about "spirit"?
In the secular vulgate, the spirit simply *does not exist*, since
secularists bow before the latest science. And science *has no
need* for the spirit. Such a word does not belong in its vocabu-
lary. What is to be done, then? Some portion—not clearly
defined—of spirit has to be taken from the "religious," from
that last letter of the acronym from which they so stubbornly
wanted to distance themselves. It is a chemical dissociation
that remains highly obscure.

The image of the tourist is generally associated with a
certain unattractiveness and awkwardness. How can this be
explained? The tourist first of all wants *to be comfortable* and
avoid the hassles of the foreign place he happens to be
visiting. Being comfortable implies a certain relaxation of
appearance. Generally the tourist wouldn't dream of wandering his own city dressed in the clothes he wears in a
foreign metropolis. Sudden changes of climate are a meager excuse. And in his choice of clothing a very clear *ani-
mus* can be detected: the emphatic statement of his own
particular lifestyle when it is thought it might be challenged

by other styles. On the other hand, the choice of the colonial English, who wore dinner jackets in the evening, corresponded to what had been their original decision: to wear the equivalent of a military uniform, making it clear that they found themselves in occupied lands.

Colonial empires have disappeared, but a deep sense of extraneousness remains, as well as hostility toward the attraction of a place. Freud felt stricken by panic in Rome due to rumors about its dangers. Over time, to overcome such embarrassments, the idea was developed about the tourist being the citizen of one state that comprises countless enclaves wedged into as many other states, where at last the inhabitants are saved from the permanent shock of extraneousness, closing themselves up in gated compounds and resorts. There, even if we come across people from other nations, we consider them first of all as belonging to a vast supranational tourist entity, to which they themselves know they belong. All of this has much to do with the forming of a category that has by now established itself as normal. It is the category of *worldwide sanctimoniousness*, the counterpart of every kind of fundamentalism.

When describing a place, people immediately say whether it is unblemished or disfigured by tourism. They talk about tourism like a skin disease. And yet the ideal tourist would like to visit places unmarred by tourism, in the same way that the ideal terrorist would like to operate in places unprotected by security measures. They both encounter certain difficulties. And have to put the blame on their fellows who have gone before them.

The convergence of cultures into one is happening in tourism and in pornography. They are parallel worlds, governed by similar rules. A maximum reduction in the range of gestures and coded actions. Minimal differences in clothing and decor. A tendency not to beat about the bush, and to avoid complicated story lines. Everything follows preset sequences. No one laughs. They get on and do it. There are no difficulties in communication, in any part of the planet. And there is no room for self-doubt in either tourism or pornography.

Strolling through the streets of an unknown city, trusting to chance, wandering toward whatever most attracts. These are now obsolete practices that very few follow. Travel now involves having a purpose: sex is the most obvious, clearly circumscribed and pragmatic. So the purpose will be the model for true innovation in tourism for the new millennium: tourism for good motives, also called "volunteer travel." Just as people *do* sex, they *do* good works. Obeying three fundamental rules: "Explore the world in a meaningful way," with the implication that traveling simply to set foot in certain places doesn't seem sufficiently meaningful. Second rule: "Travel without being a tourist." The new tourist is ashamed of being a tourist and disguises himself as something else. Third rule: "Don't just be an observer." Tourist volunteers return home with a baggage not just of films and photos but of good deeds. The secular world has no notion of grace, but it feels a continual and acute need *to save itself*. And the only other way is through earning merits, which range from educating native children to saving turtles, and culminate in a "donation." This avoids the embarrassment of giving alms to nameless beggars. Whereas the "donation" is now used for natives who are given a name. Everything has to be "meaningful." Simple enjoyment, which still takes up part of the journey, would otherwise be regarded as unbalanced, reprehensible, and bland.

The mechanism tends toward self-sufficiency: the native children who are taught something by tourist volunteers then themselves—so we are assured—tend to become part of the organization and to teach future tourist volunteers. Thus the circle is completed, involving no contact with the outside world, which can still be ignored. It is a game in which all the players are convinced they are obtaining some benefit: the promotion agency, the tourist volunteers, the natives, and the turtles. Notable among the sponsors is the Bill and Melinda Gates Foundation. No one could object, at the risk of censure. But might something be missing? Tourist volunteers are unlikely to be brushed by "a fleeting shadow of pleasure."

"The next century would allow only two types, two constitutions, two forms of reaction: those that acted and aimed high and those that kept silent awaiting metamorphosis—criminals and monks, there would be nothing else." This was what Gottfried Benn's character, the Ptolemian, prophesied. There is no shortage of criminals, the monks are invisible, but perhaps they still hold world order, like the Seven Vedic Seers or the hidden wise men of the Kabbalah. Those, however, who allow themselves to be seen are of two other kinds: tourists and terrorists.

Tourists, terrorists: ubiquitous, magnetic categories. They attract through their own force. But there are also those, as a light counterbalance, who are restive and refractory. And there always have been: a certain number—not many—of beings who can find their way through the strictures of class, of the professions, of social barriers. Who become stateless and extraterritorial by vocation. And this through no ill-will toward their fellow beings, but by trusting in a certain thrill of anonymity and the inability to feel tied to predefined roles. They are the hidden and unrecognized contemplators who have always lived in the nooks and crannies of society. In Vedic India, people would talk about the *vānaprastha*, those who go "into the forest." When the forest is no longer there, they wander in everyone's streets, but from a certain glint in their eyes it can be seen *they do not belong*.

If tourists are viewed with a certain embarrassment and a hint of disapproval, it is humanity that looks at itself and suspects it has lost something. It doesn't know exactly what, but knows it is irretrievable. Someone has suggested that democracy has extended to everyone the privilege of access to things that are no longer there.

Tourism has now skidded out of control and doesn't necessarily seem to have any more to do with travel. Rather, it looks like a second reality, which happens to be the model for virtual reality. Depleted precisely because it is augmented, like every virtual reality. If David Chalmers's statement is true that "we are not far away from a time when a virtual reality may be indistinguishable from the real thing," it must also be recognized that tourism is no longer a flourishing sector of the world, but the whole world has become a sector of tourism that has still to be brought up-to-date. This reflects on all that *is not* tourism. And which now turns out to be something depleted, as well as augmented.

Some fateful phrases say much more than they intend to say. And so, in the epilogue of the synopsis of his forthcoming book, David Chalmers announces the near future with a fanfare: "The mind starts bleeding into the world." Which can be interpreted as the mind seeping into the world, or the mind bleeding over the world. Chalmers means the first. The second is what is happening.

For theorists of virtual reality, the constant concern is to establish what difference there is between virtual reality and ordinary reality. John Searle observed that a virtual hurricane doesn't get anyone wet—and this might at first seem a conclusive observation. In response it was suggested to him that, since words can have many meanings, virtual hurricanes can be different from ordinary ones while still being hurricanes in the experience of those who suffer them.

But these are modest satisfactions. The true watershed is another. Virtual reality is focused on fighting a single enemy: Ananke, Necessity. Its aim is to elude it, thwarting it. Until one day . . . On that day, perhaps not too far off, even a virtual attack will be able to *bleed* the mind over the world.

With his protruding visor, destined to become miniaturized, like everything else, and replaced in the end by brain implants, the frequenter of virtual reality (also called *augmented reality*) is a direct descendant of the tourist who goes looking for extreme experiences. Both temporarily suspend the irreversible. The first knows he can remove his visor at any moment, the other that on a certain day he will return home. Suspending the irreversible means escaping entropy. The young Buddha followed the path in the opposite direction. He left his father's house, which seemed untouched by change, in order to encounter the irreversible in its threefold aspect of sickness, old age, and death. That, for him, was *augmented reality*. But the Buddha said only that it was reality *tathā*, "so." And he taught how to see the *tathatā*, "being so," of everything that is.

The idea of the expansion of the West across the globe doesn't originate from economic globalization, but as a project proposed by Leibniz to those powerful men of the earth whom he regarded from time to time as most congenial: Louis XIV, Charles XII, Peter the Great. Before any political and military conquest, there needed to be a convergence of ideas. The Jesuits in China were patrols reconnoitering along that way. And Leibniz wrote to one of them, Père Verjus, to explain how he wished to proceed. What might make "a great impression on the Emperor of

China and on certain intelligent people of that country"? The binary number system. This discovery by Leibniz, which then became the essential instrument for information technology, and so too for making the world function at the beginning of the twenty-first century, was already to be found in the broken and unbroken lines of the hexagrams of the *I Ching*, which Leibniz, following the Jesuits, called "characters of Fohi"—a legendary emperor—and were part of a primordial revelation. The hexagrams served to explain the state and movement of things for those who consulted that book of oracles which stands at the foundation of China. The binary number system, on the other hand, was one of various mathematical discoveries that Leibniz had happened upon.

But Leibniz had no illusion that the binary number system would be enough to establish a *communicatio idiomatum* between the West and China. He was well aware that there were radical theological disagreements. And the first of these was the Christian idea of creation from nothing. So binary numbering could serve firstly to soften the differences, demonstrating that there were also points of agreement: "It can serve to render more acceptable one of the great articles, and certainly not the easiest, of our religion and of our metaphysics, which holds that God and nothing are the origin or all things, that God has created everything from nothing."

Leibniz's global projects were unsuccessful and remained buried in exchanges of letters between scholars and in diplomatic documents. But the West lost none of its inclination to spread itself over the planet, absorbing within it as many barbarians as possible, often belonging to proud and ancient civilizations, which it could regard only as material to shape and use, thereby creating a sort of perpetual seismic shock. Leibniz had a clairvoyant view about points of convergence and what still had to be developed—and, at the same time, was clearly aware of possible theological conflicts. *Creatio ex nihilo* was indeed entirely alien to the cosmogonic conceptions of China. And Leibniz wanted to use it to investigate the possibilities of an understanding with the Chinese emperor.

Leibniz's projects are viewed today with a condescending smile. Everyone knows that things ended differently. During its expansion, the West has produced, among a multitude of other results, also a certain brutishness of thought which, instead of becoming broader, has narrowed down to its crudest terms. If it were possible to weave Leibniz's thread once again into the weft of what is taking place, at first one would notice only a minimal difference, which would yet become enormous if, by reason of some improbable effect, it could be interwoven into everything.

The Chinese emperor doesn't seem to have been much impressed by the binary number system. He kept his silence. The Chinese response to Leibniz came two centuries later, through the extraterritorial intelligence of René Guénon: "We seem to see the smile of the Chinese before this rather puerile interpretation, which, far from giving them a 'high idea of European science,' enabled them to assess its real extent. The truth is that the Chinese have never 'lost the meaning,' or rather the meanings, of these symbols; they simply didn't feel obliged to explain them to the first-comer, especially if they judged it to be a waste of effort; and Leibniz, in speaking of 'I know not what remote meanings,' admits in so many words that he understands nothing about it. These meanings, carefully preserved by tradition (which the commentaries always follow faithfully), are what constitute 'the true explanation,' and there is nothing 'mystical' about them; but what better proof of incomprehension than taking metaphysical symbols for 'purely numerical characters'? Metaphysical symbols: this is essentially what 'trigrams' and 'hexagrams' are, a synthetic representation of theories that can have unlimited developments as well as multiple adaptations if, instead of remaining in the realm of principles, they are applied to one or other specific order. Leibniz would have been most surprised if he had been told that his arithmetical interpretation was also included among those meanings which he rejected without knowing, but only on an altogether accessory and subordinate level; his interpretation, indeed, is not false in itself, it is compatible with all the others, but it is by far incomplete and insufficient, and taken by itself is devoid of meaning; it holds some interest only in virtue of the analogical correspondence that connects the lower meanings with the higher sense, in accordance with what we have said on the nature of the 'traditional sciences.' The higher sense is the pure metaphysical sense; as for the rest, they are only different applications, more or less important, but always contingent." These "different applications" are the basis on

which the world functions, in the West and in China, three
centuries after Leibniz.

An enormous mental upheaval, which no one would be
able to contain, was caused—and continues to be caused—
by the confluence of *digital* and *digitable*. Knowledge assumes the form of a single encyclopedia, in perpetual
proliferation, and generally speaking digitable. An encyclopedia that juxtaposes impeccably reliable information
with baseless information, equally accessible and on the
same level. What is digitable belongs to what is familiar and
can so be used with fond indifference. Knowledge loses
prestige and appears as though made up of items—in the
sense of headings in an encyclopedia and incontrollable,
drifting rumors or *boatos*, as they say in Portuguese. The most
fascinating—and potentially fruitful—aspect of this total
encyclopedia is the *algorithmic chaos*, so that once the most
probable connections have been reached, they become increasingly arbitrary and misleading, as is supposed to happen
in a neural network. It is an invitation to enter a forest—a
mental forest, which can be seen at the same time on a
screen. But this doesn't happen. Indeed, the randomness of
knowledge in general is thus confirmed.

There is then another aspect, no less disturbing, about
the *availability of information technology*. Anyone can produce
words and images, unrestricted, publishable more or less
anywhere, for an unlimited audience. This has been enough
to arouse popular delusions of omnipotence, though no
longer as a clinical complaint. On the contrary, as an en-

hancement of normality. Mythomania has become part of common sense.

The transposition of the universe into digital form and its availability at the touch of a finger are facts unprecedented in the history of *Homo sapiens* and affect the remotest and darkest regions of mental activity. In a certain way, they are symmetrically opposite to those regions of the mind that mnemotechnical theaters sought to access. What is happening in the opening years of the third millennium can be understood only in the context of this ongoing tidal wave.

Brimming with noble sentiments, secular humanists look back at the past like Khrushchev at the countless victims of Stalin. Like him, they seem to be saying: "Just be patient, we will rehabilitate you all." But there is something else that worries them, a modest, obliging, home-reared power: information. Which has now raised its little head and stares at them with a cold, piercing gaze. As if to say: "I do not need you." Scraps of information, multiplying nonstop in every direction, turn out in the end to be self-sufficient. And capable of expanding with no help from anything external. They don't have to go through the process of thought. Big Data, itself, is the one that thinks on behalf of and looks after those who have created it. If intelligence is what is found in algorithms, then its place of preference will no longer be the mind. Indeed, the mind will tend to become the material on which those algorithms are applied. Information tends to replace not only knowledge, but thought in general, relieving it of the burden of having to continually rework and govern itself.

Information, by encircling thought, basically suffocates it. It is an inflation of Hermes, which at the same time mutilates the shape of the god, canceling his role as companion of souls and guide to the realm of all that is invisible. What remains is a sneering and fraudulent Hermes, lavisher of poisoned gifts. First among these is the promise to get rid of intermediaries. An operation that finally allows everyone to show their intolerance of representation.

There is always someone ready to scorn representation. Or at least to rage about the fact that all representation is a falsification and doesn't render full justice to the individuality of the person represented. But there are also those sober and clear-sighted people who have seen that this is how we are made and that every representation must be seen as a mediation. This in turn has aroused a certain distrust and suspicion toward every element or person that acts as intermediary. For it was there, according to some, that deception and eventual betrayal lurked.

Until one day, at the dawn of the digital world, an intriguing word appeared: *disintermediation*. It was now enough to tap in a certain sequence of words and anyone would have the impression of acting for themselves, without resorting to the usual tiresome intermediaries. If this was true for a journey or a hotel booking, why couldn't it also be true for politics? It is a question that has confused many—and continues to do so as digitality spreads and disintermediation offers cheap thrills at every step. On closer observation,

disintermediation turns out to be based on a hatred of mediation. Which is fatal for thought. We don't need to go back
to Hegel to realize that not only thought but also perception
exists only by virtue of mediation, therefore through continual adjustments and compromises, which are what mediation is all about. Even the mirage of direct democracy now
comes, not from political reflection, but from an infatuation
with information technology. Which, by debasing mediation, ends up also debasing immediacy, attainable only
after having crossed the lattice of mediations.

If intelligence has been absorbed into nonconscious algorithms that yet function more effectively than the mind—a
shorthand description of the information revolution—it is
easy to imagine then, as a next step, that *consciousness* should
undergo something similar. But it is here that we encounter an unexpected obstacle. Intelligence can be seen as a
succession of discrete states which can in principle be sim-
ulated even outside the mind. But consciousness? Here,
despite the abundance of works that deal with it, one crip-
pling observation is unavoidable: no one knows what consciousness is actually made of. And not only do we not
know, but every tool that ought to help us understand it,
such as fMRI or three-dimensional microscopy, only in-
tensifies our own sense of inadequacy. And yet we are
convinced that consciousness is an entity present in all
humans, even if we have some difficulty proving it, whereas
for intelligence we can offer lots of tests. Consciousness is
the invisible barrier against which information collides.
This is the single humiliating blow that has to be faced by

that power accustomed to spreading in all directions. And which is obviously ready to continue spreading, in spite of all humiliation.

Deviant and disruptive grandchildren of secular humanists, transhumanists—a variegated band that gathers under the flag of Ray Kurzweil's Singularity—are convinced that death is a prejudice to be done away with. In this respect they are not unlike typical social democrats, according to whom all problems have a solution, so long as a reasonable amount of time is given to resolve them. And here already the waters of thought divide. Gödel's major discovery was to show how certain problems can *never* be resolved. The crucial point is to identify what these problems are. The fact that arithmetic was the first among all of them can also be seen as an indication that these were questions of fundamental importance. And nothing is more fundamental than death.

But transhumanists are not to be frightened off. They believe they hold a card that is valid for every game: technology, along with credulity. For them, everything is a matter of implementing more than of thinking. This is the mirage they head toward, impatient, lugubrious, and blithe. A mirage obliquely connected to those, in antiquity, who wanted to transform spiritual achievements into as many powers.

Transhumanists, though lacking any sense of the divine, feel an acute attraction toward what was promised by religion, in its various manifestations. And it was always the promise of some kind of salvation. But this can no longer be contained in a ritual form: it has to become palpable. A pitiful error—to manipulate the invisible. Which becomes elusive and slips away.

With the emergence of tranhumanists, secularists have revealed what had always been their purpose: not to abandon religion but to absorb it, using it for their own ends. This was always their occult plan, which can now be openly expressed, thanks to technology. Previously, the means were lacking.

The move from Dadaism to Dataism, from Dada to Big Data, happened over exactly a century. And there are those who claim that Big Data will supplant Sapiens and drag him helplessly along like a straw in the mighty flow of information. We will then be close to knowing almost everything we don't need to know. Whereas new kinds of algorithms will certainly know how to reap the benefits.

Dataism may come to be regarded one day as an instance of mass delirium, like the teachings of the Reverend Jim Jones. But that day is not close at hand. Not only is a large part of what is happening moving in that direction, but a not insignificant part of humanity is happy that this is so. There is clearly someone yearning for a new "religion" who feels happy to be told that "the supreme value of this new religion is 'information flow.'" At this point *Homo saecularis*, with his noble humanistic values, will feel as obsolete as a beguine of ancient times.

Dada was the moment of universal disjunction, declared and pursued through a systematic erosion of meaning (and this corresponded with a disjunction acted out during the years 1914–1918). Dataism is the moment of compulsory connection, which eliminates all that eludes it and where everyone becomes a proud and irrelevant silicon soldier in an army whose leaders are nowhere to be found—if indeed there are any leaders.

Homo becomes enormously more powerful if he simulates himself, imitating himself in an incomplete and imperfect way. If he were able instead to produce identical copies, he would remain as he is. And this is one of his supreme quirks. Turing's machine is so powerful because it imitates the process of the mind as if it were a succession of discrete states, whereas this is not the case. And Turing himself said this.

A key word in this respect is *simulation*. It appears all the more significant if there are those transhumanists who replace it with *emulation*, even developing, like Randal Koene, an "*emulation project*." The purpose behind the move is euphemistic, since it is possible in this way to remove the connotation of *falsity* that is inextricably linked to simulation. But in fact the situation is worsened, rather than improved, since emulation thrusts the competitive characteristic of imitation into the forefront. And, with this, its implicit violence. The emulator is the most fearsome enemy, since his aim is to take the place of the person he models himself on, not subjugating but eliminating him.

The religion of Dataism, according to Yuval Noah Harari, is based on these dogmas: "Humanism thought that experiences occur inside us, and that we ought to find within ourselves the meaning of all that happens, thereby infusing the universe with meaning. Dataists believe that experiences are valueless if they are not shared, and that we need not—indeed *cannot*—find meaning within ourselves. We need only record and connect our experience to the great data flow, and the algorithms will discover its meaning and tell us what to do." Harari, like Bentham, belongs to those beings who have the gift of saying with brutal clarity what many others don't realize they already think—and would not dare to formulate. We must be grateful to such beings, for they allow us to know exactly what we are dealing with.

Compared with the old Bentham, who had very little in the way of doubt, the new Bentham manages to incorporate doubt into his demonstration. Having described the inevitable emptying of everything into the "cosmic data flow," Harari casually allows a deadly observation to fall: in twenty years, "maybe we'll discover that organisms aren't algorithms after all." The phrase is nonchalantly thrown in, but its consequences are devastating. So Dataism could be one of those long-lasting errors: "Many previous religions gained enormous popularity and power despite their factual mistakes. If Christianity and communism could do it, why not Dataism?" Yet it is still difficult to evaluate Christianity in terms of its "factual mistakes." Perhaps the absence of proof for the resurrection of the flesh?

But the true esoteric arguments come at the end and are incisive: "In the past, censorship worked by blocking the flow of information. In the twenty-first century, censorship works by flooding people with irrelevant information." A notion from which there is a corollary: "Today having power means knowing what to ignore." It is a gloss to a new Machiavelli—and as such it has to be taken seriously.

Gregory Chaitin had just written several blunt and concise lines on binary arithmetic: "Leibniz sensed in the 0 and 1 bits the combinatorial power to create the entire universe, which is exactly what happens in modern digital electronic computers and the rest of our digital information technology. [. . .] It's all 0's and 1's, that's our entire image of the world! You just combine 0's and 1's, and you get everything." And at that very moment he came across a review in the January 2004 issue of *Nature*, where Michael Nielsen, "coauthor of the large and authoritative *Quantum Computation and Quantum Information*," wrote: "What is the Universe made of? A growing number of scientists suspect that information plays a fundamental role in answering this question. Some even go as far as to suggest that information-based concepts may eventually fuse with or replace traditional notions such as particles, fields or forces. The Universe may literally be made of information, they say, an idea neatly encapsulated in physicist John Wheeler's slogan: 'It from bit.' [. . .] These are speculative ideas, still in the early days of development."

Chaitin agreed. Without intending to do so, in those few lines, Nielsen had set out the manifesto of the digital era, whose supreme aspiration is to reach full and ubiquitous control of the *discrete,* using *information* as its emissary and plenipotentiary. Back in 2004, of course, they were "speculative ideas, still in the early days of development." And it was a period of torrid development. Today, the title of the new book by David Chalmers is *Its from Bits.* Wheeler's slogan has obviously become the banner for those who want to trace the whole of nature back to one single power: the discrete. Banished from "Cantor's paradise," where the continuous still reigned, even in its more disturbing aspects, Homo is tempted to build himself a new paradise, populated only by boundless multitudes of bits. Ignoring outright the constitution of conscious life, which could not exist without the continuous.

Behind Wheeler's motto, and likewise behind Nielsen's involuntary manifesto, could be glimpsed a hazardous plan: substituting bits for real numbers, toward which "mathematicians [. . .] have always had a slightly queasy attitude." Chaitin immediately recognized the obstacle encountered by this fatal step: "A real number isn't a digital object, it's an analog object. And since it varies continuously, not in discrete jumps, if you convert such a number into bits you get an infinite number of bits. But computers can't perform computations with numbers that have an infinite number of bits!" It would seem an insuperable obstacle. Yet Chaitin wasn't so easily defeated. And he immediately introduced a crucial doubt, asking "whether the physical world is really continuous or whether it might actually be discrete, like some rebels are beginning to suspect." A question that has meanwhile become a burning issue among physicists, to the point that there are now more "rebels" in the continuous camp than in the discrete camp. In any event, apart from theoretical disputes about the functioning of the world, the supremacy of the discrete has become overwhelming. And the "rebels" are now the scattered tribes of the analogical, with their vinyl records.

When Chaitin set out his algorithmic information theory in the 1960s, his ideas bore the fragrance of the new, and no one imagined that *algorithm* would have become the first obsessive word of the impending millennium, or that *information* would be its eagle-eyed sovereign. As sometimes—rarely—happens, a scientific theory was also the early symptom of an anthropological mutation.

For science there is not yet an adequate, all-inclusive definition of *information*—and still less an adequate definition of *consciousness*. They are two entities we have to deal with all the time, without being able to say what they are. The relationship between information and consciousness can also be seen as an episode of the alternation, superimposition, and conflict between discrete and continuous that takes place perpetually in the whole of nature. And, under analogical and digital guise, it appears as an essential characteristic of our nervous system. Von Neumann identified it with the greatest clarity in that slim book, *The Computer and the Brain*, which is the griffin on the threshold of computer science. But the question had been posed much earlier. According to Simone Weil, "since Greece, science is a sort of dialogue between the continuous and the discontinuous." An inevitable dialogue because "the discontinuous and the continuous are givens of the human mind, which necessarily thinks one and the other; and it is natural that it goes from one to the other." But it is a dialogue that can also turn into war. And war tends to manifest itself above all as an invasion of territories. Something can then happen that "is repugnant to reason, namely that the discontinuous is applied to magnitudes essentially continuous. And this is the case with time and space." Over seventy years later, the majority of physicists would disagree with Weil on this point.

But there is another territory where the discrete has conducted a relentless invasion, encountering only scarce resistance: the territory of the mind, as well as that of consciousness. An invasion accompanied by impressive empirical results, which have an effect on everyone's lives. Even more radical has been the upheaval that has happened as a result in conceptions about mind and consciousness, both of which are now attached to the territory of the discrete. This is the hidden dividing line that marks out the distance between the new and the past millennium. And there are no indications that the nascent empire is prepared to recognize that it is founded on such a stubborn, lethal misinterpretation.

Information can only be discrete. Consciousness is a shapeless blend of discrete and continuous, but that same shapelessness places it on the side of the continuous. It belongs to a non–self-sufficient substratum, incised by various orifices, through which it breathes and evacuates, depending at every moment on the outside world. Information is basically autistic. It needs only a plug point, and therefore presupposes a social order that can provide a constant and safe supply of energy. Similar in this respect to the main *desideratum* of transhumanists: a life prolonged indefinitely, so as to soften every residual tragic feeling about existence, a life that would be occupied by an incessant whirl of bits, in every angle of consciousness. With transhumanism, experimental society nears its final and perfect form: not to experiment only on itself, as an all-embracing entity, but on each of its components, however minuscule.

And here the moment approaches when *values*, which have already done so much damage, are readying themselves to be introduced even into machines. Stuart Russell, author of the most widely read treatise on artificial intelligence, looks with concern at the time, in the near future, when robots will have left humans behind in terms of intelligence and will start to consider them *redundant.* There's a joke in the AI world about certain inventive gorillas that one day fashion man and then discover that they themselves are still gorillas. What to do? Create doubt, uncertainty in robots. Make them humble. Teach them not to follow programs *too literally.* In this way they will come to represent a "human-compatible" artificial intelligence. In this way, a beneficial "value alignment" will be created, and—among other things—the robot will become "altruistic." In this way, by—hopefully—becoming good robots (now definable as "beneficial machines"), humans will also find an opportunity to *improve themselves*.

But wasn't it precisely this age-old sentiment that, according to Adam Smith, accompanied man from the cradle to the grave? "The principle which prompts to save, is the desire of bettering our condition, a desire which, though generally calm and dispassionate, comes with us from the womb, and never leaves us till we go into the grave. In the whole interval which separates those two moments, there is scarce perhaps a single instant in which any man is so perfectly and compleatly satisfied with his situation, as to be without any wish of alteration or improvement of any kind." Investors in artificial intelligence can therefore rest assured: not only are they bringing benefit, making humans better, but they are following *to the letter* the dictates of the founding father of political economy.

In his TED Talk of April 25, 2017, Stuart Russell announced another important point that will be developed in his forthcoming book. How can the superintelligent robot be made to find its way around human *values*? A difficult but—as usual—resolvable question. Until very recently Russell had indicated what the objective of "Human-Compatible AI" had to be. But it wasn't clear how it ought to operate. Like all his colleagues, Russell was expecting that a massive quantity of data would have been enough to resolve the problem. An extremely generic solution. Now he seems to have had the inspiration that gives the exact *modus operandi* to be followed: *the machine has to learn to read.* Read what? Everything. It will read "every-thing the human race has ever written." Just a few words, but enough to present a horror that no science-fiction story had managed to evoke: a vast mass of signs in every type of alphabet that are read by a robot and from which gushes, like a smooth syrup, the essence of *values.*

A person's inclination to expose himself to the shock of the unknown is a secret and cherished sensation, which says much about the quality of such a person. There are those who ignore it, and those who cannot resist it. In any event it is an archaic vestige. In a very remote age, before prehistory, that sensation was a constant experience. Today its presence is felt when we approach a site of ruins, one of those silent and enclosed places that evoke the past through fragments of stone. Many visitors want or love or expect to be accompanied there by guides or audio guides. Others wander such places as though blind. They will see the place—if they ever see it at all—only through what they have recorded through a lens. And above all, what they see again will be themselves. Then there are those who simply look. Among these few, there are some—a meager sect—determined to lay themselves open to the shock of the unknown. They know it to be an invaluable sensation and preliminary to all con-nection with the past. That sensation is like the first stage of a rite of initiation that takes place in darkness and silence. But it is essential in order to establish a relationship with the unknown. Which, in the case of the past, is above all absence. Ruins bear witness to this: that the past is not there. Having once absorbed this shock, which penetrates deep into the veins, the process of knowledge can then—slowly, gradually—begin. Great historians are necromancers—and so too are visitors. They have all undergone that initial experience, which keeps happening again, even if their physiologies may be very different: austere, as in the case of Burckhardt—or visionary, as with Michelet.

Digitability is the gravest infliction for those inclined to lay themselves open to the shock of the unknown. That sensation was cultivated by few, like a secret. But the Web has obliged everyone to assume a vast weight of learning that they do not know, as though engulfed from every direction by an uninterrupted and instructive whir. A Google Earth extended over time suffocates any perception of the unknown, which is inevitably mitigated and weakened— or eventually neutralized.

There is also the possibility of sitting on the shore of the great data flow, without complaint and without apology. With no obligation to meditate, with no duty to perform good deeds, without worrying too much about what one eats or drinks. Limiting oneself to practicing what in itself is self-fulfilling. And looking, while including the observer himself in what is being looked at. Cautiously to try to inquire whether the one looking is our guest or whether it is we who are his guests. Letting him go first and giving a nod of agreement.

"Even if Kafka did not pray—and this we do not know—he still possessed in the highest degree what Malebranche called 'the natural prayer of the soul': attention.

And in this attention he included all living creatures, as saints include them in their prayers." Adorno was deeply struck by these words of Walter Benjamin and immediately in a letter he referred to the "enormous definition of attention as an historical figure of prayer." That definition of Malebranche applied what Benjamin had evoked fifty years before, under the name of "profane illumination." A formula that could have become the first axiom of his *secularized theology*, whose founding charter instead remained hidden in the recesses of his essay on surrealism. It consisted of few words: "It doesn't take us very far to stress, with pathos or with fanaticism, the enigmatic aspect of what is enigmatic; on the contrary, we penetrate mystery only to the degree that we recognize it in the everyday realm, by virtue of a dialectical point of view that perceives the everyday as impenetrable and the impenetrable as everyday." It was a premise charged with an immense potential energy—and Benjamin gave several examples of how to apply it. Reading became a particular case of telepathy. Thought was an expansion of the intoxication from hashish. And so too someone who is waiting, or the *flâneur*, or the dreamer, or someone who has taken a drug, each became profane illuminati. And prayer another name for attention.

All of this could result in an upheaval that Benjamin condensed into a formula: "To win the force of intoxication for the revolution." If there was ever a contribution by Benjamin to any revolution, it was this phrase. When he wrote it, Benjamin didn't yet know that the only revolution dear to him—the one in Russia—was involving itself in something quite different. But the idea of a *secularized theology*, which has obsessed and besieged the whole twentieth century, did not wear itself out for this. Anyone who thinks beyond the bounds of logic and mathematics knows that theological categories are always alive and at work. At the same time, once beyond a certain threshold of history, certain gestures become irreversibly obliterated. Thinking is pointless, unless there is an attempt to think about the nature of *sacrifice*. But it is unthinkable now to practice blood sacrifice in any form. Something could be said along the same lines about other theological notions, such as *grace* and *free will*. Which are now taken away from their religious context and scattered like dolmens over a vast wild and silent landscape.

When K. emerges from the mist that cloaks the village beneath the Castle, he enters a new normality, which has nothing extraordinary or supernatural. But it is incongruous, ludicrous, elusive. K. feels the powers and is not sure what to call them. Everything, depending on the moment and point of view, could be benevolent or malevolent.

The more insubstantial the world is, the more people there are to complain about it. But even their complaint is insubstantial. Robert Frost examined the difference between "grievances" and "griefs" in his introduction to a posthumous collection by E. A. Robinson, a poet he much admired: "Grievances are a form of impatience. Griefs are a form of patience. We may be required by law to throw away patience as we have been required to surrender gold;

since by throwing away patience and joining the impatient in one last rush on the citadel of evil, the hope is we may end the need of patience. There will be nothing left to be patient about. The day of perfection waits on unanimous social action. Two or three more good national elections should do the business. It has been similarly urged on us to give up courage, make cowardice a virtue, and see if that won't end war, and the need of courage. Desert religion for science, clean out the holes and corners of the residual unknown, and there will be no more need of religion. (Religion is merely consolation for what we don't know.) But suppose there was some mistake; and the evil stood siege, the war didn't end, and something remained unknowable. Our having disarmed would make our case worse than it had ever been before. Nothing in the latest advices from Wall Street, the League of Nations, or the Vatican inclines me to give up my holdings in patient grief." It was the definitive response to all pacifism and to all grievances about the way of the world.

Let us imagine a European finding himself in London and strolling through the city late one afternoon. He may happen to pass in front of the British Museum. Swarms of people, from every country, who enter and leave. He may join those who enter: there's not even an entrance charge. Just inside the museum are various shops selling souvenirs and postcards. Then there's a turn through a door to the left. The Rosetta Stone, Egyptian and Assyrian statues. And then a room containing a strange construction. Columns, reliefs, and several statues of headless female beings that seem suspended in air. There are various exhibit labels. It is the Nereid Monument. From Xanthos, in Lycia. Present-day southern Turkey. The descriptions are incomplete. The date: fourth century before Christ. But Lycia—what is Lycia? And what was the origin of the monument, described as an early example of a temple-tomb? The explanations given in the museum relate to events that took place in a part of Asia Minor about which very little is known. But is it really Asia? Or do those hovering figures, with pleated swathes that shape their bodies, belong to something else? Why don't they have the rigidity of all the other figures, Egyptian or Assyrian, displayed just a few meters away? Why do they evoke an idea of *softness* that is not necessarily connected to stability and solemnity? These are just some of the questions raised by the Nereid Monument. But, among the questions, an unexpected answer creeps in. That temple-tomb is Europe. Or at least: it is something that acquires its meaning only when linked to Europe. And it wasn't even found in Europe, but inland from the Turkish southern coast. Princess Europa herself had also come from Lebanon.

II

THE VIENNA
GAS COMPANY

These are not recollections. They are words written, published, spoken, recounted, recorded during the period from early January 1933 to May 1945. They all have an unintentionally familiar ring. Each image of those years, whatever its origin, has something hypnotic about it. This was the peak of black and white, in cinema and in life. When Technicolor appeared it seemed a hallucination. Time seemed to have been shaped into an ever narrower spiral, which ended in a bottleneck.

January 30, 1933. Klaus Mann leaves Berlin in the early morning, "as though urged by a bad omen." Roads empty. City asleep. "It was to be my last sight of Berlin, the farewell." A stop at Leipzig. His friend Erich Ebermayer emerges from the station. Pale, agitated. " 'What's going on?' I asked. He seemed surprised: 'What, you don't know? The old man's appointed him an hour ago.' 'The old man? . . . *Who's* appointed?' 'Hitler. He's Chancellor.' "

1933. Hitler's Germany arrived in France with the sound of the radio, which was functioning badly, emitting "fearful gurgling sounds." Only in 1932 had it managed to become "a well organized scourge," almost for one event alone. Robert Brasillach and his friends were listening in: "Everything was ready so that we could hear, that evening, tuning in to the German channels, that extraordinary electoral campaign of national-socialism, stream of bells, of drums, of violins, unleashing of all the demons of music."

Six years later, when Brasillach was writing his recollections as a thirty-year-old in uniform, 1933 now appeared in a light that was both distant and menacing: "In the sequence of our youthful years, the year 1933 perhaps doesn't appear clearest to us. On the contrary, it is blurred, now pallid now tinted, with that ghostly and cawing aspect of Edgar Poe's raven perched on the bust of Pallas that crucial moments easily assume in our memory. This was indeed the most crucial year of all, the one we were waiting for without knowing it from when we were casting an eye around us, always pursuing our personal, live and sweet and wise adventure. It arrived in the end, dark and striped with glares, suddenly loud then dull and muffled, and barely could we separate it from our forecasts, from our expectations, so much was it still mixed up with them, and yet it was the mysterious year of fulfillment and of threat."

March 12, 1933. The editors of *Voilà* commissioned Georges Simenon to write a series of articles from various European countries. They told him: "Europe is sick. The doctor bends down, puts his ear to the patient's heart: 'Say 33.' And the patient repeats '33 . . . 33 . . . 33.'"

Simenon starts off in Warsaw, where it is snowing: "The

snow muffles the footsteps and the voices. The snow muffles the conflict. It has a face of peace. And yet, hereabout, there are some who worry, who are imperceptibly anxious in case . . .

"In case tomorrow, when the snow has melted and the earth has turned black and teeming, there should be a rush toward newly visible frontiers.

"This is no business of mine. I left with a more modest purpose, to see the face of Europe today. There was a Europe before 1914, then a Europe carved by trenches, and finally a postwar Europe.

"But isn't there perhaps yet another Europe, the Europe of 1933, which slumbers beneath the snow and, like a restless sleeper, has sudden spasms, which frighten us?"

March 20, 1933. Walter Benjamin writes to Gershom Scholem that the latest urge to leave Germany has come from the "almost mathematical simultaneousness with which practically all the centers I was in contact with have returned my manuscripts, have broken off negotiations pending or almost ripe for completion." Germany has become the country where "when talking to someone you fix your eyes on the lapels of their jackets, preferring not to look anyone in the face anymore."

April 29, 1933. Bored by her corrections to "that silly book" *Flush*, Virginia Woolf noted her impressions of Bruno Walter, whom she had just met: "He is a swarthy, fattish, man; not at all smart. Not at all the 'great conductor.' He is a little Slav, a little semitic. He is very nearly mad; that is, he cant get 'the poison' as he called it of Hitler out of him. 'You must not think of the Jews' he kept saying. 'You must think of this awful reign of intolerance. You must think of the whole state of the world. It is terrible—terrible. That this meanness, that this pettiness, should be possible! Our Germany—which I loved—without our tradition—our culture—We are now a disgrace.' Then he told us how you cant talk above a whisper. There are spies everywhere. He had to sit in the window of his hotel in Leipzig? a whole day, telephoning. All the time soldiers were marching. They never stop marching. And on the wireless, between the turns, they play military music." Woolf adds: "He has the intensity—genius?—which makes him live every thing he feels."

Spring 1933. Erika Irrgang, Cillie Ambor, Anny Angel, Annie Reich: Céline's Mittel-European galaxy of girl-friends. To whom he was affectionate, protective. Every so often he visited them, trying to disturb their lives as little as he could. Every so often, from a distance, he tried to direct their traffic of other lovers. He gave plenty of suggestions on how to avoid getting pregnant. Sodomy was the solution he recommended. Cillie was Jewish and Céline was concerned about her: "I wonder if you are safe in Vienna, whether Hitlerism isn't also going to invade Austria." And a few days later: "I'm very pleased to know that for the moment you are safe but *la folie hitler* will end up dominating Europe for several centuries yet. Mr. Freud can do nothing about it."

May 8, 1933. Martin du Gard meets Henry de Montherlant, who has just got off a ship from Algeria, disgusted by the ex-servicemen who were with him on board. They were returning from a congress with their wives and did everything they could not to pay for their drinks at the bar. The conversation moves on to the rise of National Socialism: "I have always refused to go to Germany since the war, Montherlant tells me; and yet I was persuaded that the new life . . . yes, that the life was there. Today I don't want to go there because, at this moment, I would like it too much."

May 1933. Céline writes to Eugène Dabit: "There's a *je ne sais quoi* in the air . . . There's molting—It's a boat sailing into the distance . . . We're heading toward violence. It's extremely close." The horror that was coming into view, the *new* horror, wasn't just the totalitarian one—a euphemistic term, a temporary delimitation. The horror wasn't just a certain form of society, but society itself, in that finally it admitted to being self-sufficient, sovereign, and devouring under whatever form. People would one day rid themselves of Hitler and of Stalin, but not of society. Céline, who did not work by reasoning but by intuition, and immediately eclipsed the intuition he had just had, wrote to Élie Faure: "We are all indeed absolutely dependent on our Society. It is it that decides our destiny." For once, he had even used a capital *S*.

May 22, 1933. Joseph Roth gets angry, urging his friend Stefan Zweig to leave his publisher, the noble Insel Verlag

("I have the impression you overvalue the moral qualities of Insel Verlag"). The publisher, Anton Kippenberg, had recently authorized certain stylistic corrections in the *völkisch*, "national-popular," therefore National Socialist manner, in Zweig's book on Marie Antoinette, without notifying the author. But Roth's concerns went further: "I fear, so to speak, for the health of your soul. May I speak with total frankness? I fear you haven't yet fully understood what is happening. You continue to think about it. You continue to 'clarify.'

"This is my opinion:

a) it lasts four years;

b) Hitler ends in disaster or in monarchy;

c) there's no relationship *at all* between us and the Third Reich;

d) in five months' time there'll be no publisher, no bookseller, no author of our kind;

e) we have to *abandon* all hope, finally, firmly, strongly, as is fitting. Between us and him there is war. Any thought for the enemy is punished with death. All major writers who have remained here will suffer literary death;

f) so long as we are banned, no contact with those of the 'Left.' Feuchtwanger, A. Zweig, Weltbühne. They too are to blame for our fate. It's the party of arrogant fools."

1933. This is how Ernst Jünger appears to Martin du Gard, who pays him a visit in Berlin: "A boy of thirty-five, with ascetic face, full of energy and reserve, sporting, dressed for golf, plus fours, a cigarette between his lips." As he speaks, there emerges the "total Nietzschean who would happily refuse to enter the *Reichswehr* because they don't have a sufficiently high conception of sacrifice; a fervent heart, hard, or rather hardened, over and above all appetites, and who inspires respect." Jünger's disconsolate exclamation follows: "We have lost everything, even honor!" It is accompanied by an analysis: "The movement of the masses has gone, he tells me, personal valor is imposed in Russia and in Italy. And it must be imposed in Germany. But the socialist ideal is not dead. Social democracy is no longer capable of being the agent of socialism. It is now the turn of the National Socialists . . ."

December 25, 1933. On Christmas Day, Jörg Lanz von Liebenfels completes a short essay entitled "The Primordial Electric God and His Great Sanctuary in Prehistoric Times." On the cover of the booklet was a summary of the text: "Content: the 'gods' are no more than pre-human beings electrically organized ('electrozoa'), the rediscovery of God through radiology and serology, God is heroic stock, his religious laws are laws of racial breeding, primitive man as pet of the angels and of the Valkyries, the rediscovery of the original homeland of the electric Griffins, of the Valkyries, of swan-girls and angels in the territory of Rügen, the secret sanctuary, 'the laboratory of noble ancestry and the maternal womb of the people,' the mysterious 'oracular doves' (= Valkyries!) of the ancient temples, Asclepius's 'cockerels of lightning,' the electric 'amber,' the road of 'amber,' the land of 'amber,' the original homeland of the Aryan heroes and heroic sagas, the birthplace of Aryo-heroic humanity and of the original Christian religion of racial breeding and of the religion of the Grail."

On another Christmas Day, twenty-six years before, at Werfenstein Castle, Lanz von Liebenfels had for the first time hoisted a flag with the swastika, red on a black background, with four lilies, on the occasion of a meeting of his Ordo Novi Templi (ONT) sect. Its members included August Strindberg.

January 1934. Pierre Drieu La Rochelle guesses the timing: "War breaks out, in five years. France and Germany pounce one on the other." And Russia? "Though up against Japan, Russia marches on Germany. This because Germany (Hitlerian or not) is a much greater danger for Russia than any other human group. Germany is still the big neighbor for Russia whose technological superiority is not destroyed. And then, between the semi-socialism of the German fascists and the semi-fascism of the Russian communists there is the same stubborn family hatred as between the imperialism of the Romanovs and that of the Hohenzollerns and the Habsburgs. On both sides, the same strong national base and above all the same tendency toward world evangelization. Which leads to conflict." Everything fits, except that the imperial dynasties demanded fewer corpses than the Nazi "semi-socialism" and the Soviet "semi-fascism." Times have changed.

March–April 1934. Political tensions escalate, Élie Faure tends toward the Left. But Céline can't agree, even though he writes to Faure: "You are one of my rare masters—and certainly the most intimate, the most direct." What is the real motive? Certainly not that Céline declares himself "forever an anarchist." That word, for him, is just a misleading intimation of his *nonadherence* to anything. Looking around, Céline sees himself surrounded by nothing but enemies, in all directions. Why? Everybody, to Left and Right, is talking about the "new man." But Céline writes: "I speak out loudly and strongly, passionately, against all our common rotten filth *of Man*, to the Left or the Right. And for this they will never forgive me." There is no call for theories. This fundamental perception of what is wrong in the human being is quite enough. And so the prospect of persecution is already there: "Maybe one or other will shoot me. The Nazis loathe me as much as the Socialists, and the communards too, not to mention Henri de Régnier or Comoedia or Stavisky. They're all in agreement when it comes to spitting me out. All is allowed except *to doubt Man*. On that, no jokes are allowed."

May 31, 1934. The postcard showed part of a pool, a wide, noble stairway, and the grand avenue of the Parc de Saint-Cloud, lined with lush trees, with foliage that leaned almost to the ground, as in a Fragonard. The message (in English) read: "That's where I pass my sundays now—sick of St-Germain as you may well imagine. Louis." Louis was Céline. It was addressed to Miss Elizabeth Craig, Los Angeles.

He had met her ("chatted me up," Elizabeth would one day recall) eight years earlier at the window of a bookshop in Geneva. Elizabeth was peering at a book. Céline started a conversation. He was well practiced. Elizabeth was twenty-four, tawny-blond hair. The poise of a ballerina, Céline's favorite type. Obvious, impressive beauty. She had been a pupil of Theodore Kosloff at the Imperial Russian Ballet, had danced with the Ziegfeld Follies, had appeared as an extra, with a dozen other dancing girls, in a pagan orgy scene in Cecil B. DeMille's *Manslaughter*, and had made her first trip to Paris with the Rockettes dance company. Céline's name at that time was Destouches: he was working as a doctor at the League of Nations. Soon they were living together in rue Lepic, Montmartre. It lasted seven years, the years of *Voyage*, dedicated "à Elisabeth Craig." Then, one day in 1933, Elizabeth went back to the United States—and decided not to live any longer with Céline. The postcard with the Parc de Saint-Cloud was a presentiment of that distance that Céline could not imagine and had been prefigured still earlier in the overwhelming, harrowing farewell from Molly in *Voyage au bout de la nuit*.

February 17, 1935. Robert Frost writes to Louis Untermeyer, who had won a prize awarded by the Italian Tourist Board for a book that would encourage tourism in Italy. The prize had been split equally between Untermeyer's stories and "a three-volume glorification of Mussolini." Frost observed, in passing: "I hate to be caught touring with the tourists and seeing only what is advertised to be seen." He tried to go only to places where "there were no trip tickets to it." He then went on to comment about an article by Archibald MacLeish where it was claimed that "the originality of today in art is the revolution of tomorrow in politics." Frost objected: "Tell me any poetic or belle lettre originality of any day that became the revolution of any day following." But he knew very well that the word *revolution* still had an irresistible fragrance. So he added: "If you want to play with the word revolution, every day and every new poem of a poet is a revolution of the spirit: that is to say it is a freshening." Untermeyer loathed publishers, those traders who don't know how to recognize "originality." Here too, Frost knew how to adjust his aim: "The artist's object is to tell people what they haven't as yet realized they were about to say themselves. First they are displeased, then they are pleased at this for psychological reasons we won't go into. The publisher comes in right there to help in the transition between their being displeased and pleased."

April 22, 1935. Leonard and Virginia Woolf had planned a journey by motorcar to Italy, passing through Germany. But, given all they had heard, they first wanted to talk to R. F. Wigram, a member of the Foreign Office who had been posted to Berlin. It was always wise to know how matters were viewed by the Foreign Office: "The Wigrams to tea; she in white checks, checked shoes, yellow curls, blue eyes, disappointed, embittered, growing old, growing fat, something like an old daisy or other simple garden flower; if a flower could look very unhappy. I suppose the deformed boy, & so on. He a cripple, with iron rods down one leg, hoisting himself about on a stick. This, I suppose, faintly disgusting physically to her. I suppose she lives with physical deformity. But she is too painted &

powdered, too insipidly discontented. He is very white toothed, blue eyed, lean, red cheeked—a nice rigid honest public school Englishman. Started almost at once telling us about Hitler. He had been at Berlin with Simon. Got there early & stood at the Embassy window watching the crowd. They clustered, & a policeman held up his hand, & they obediently fell back. No resistance. Then the conversations began. Hitler very impressive; very frightening. A large picture of the Madonna & Child & one of Bismarck. He has a great jowl like Bismarck. Made speeches lasting 20 minutes with out a failure. Very able. Only one mistake on a complicated point. Very well coached. And all the time a tapping sound. Wigram thought An odd day to have the masons in. But it was the sentry marching up & down the passage. Everything came out. We want . . . We have a parity in the air already. The Germans in fact have enough aeroplanes ready to start to keep us under. But if they do kill us all? Well they will have their Colonies. I want room to move about Hitler said. Must be equal, & so on. A complete reversal to pre-war days. No ideals except equality, superiority, force, possessions. And the passive heavy slaves behind him, and he a great mould coming down on the brown jelly. Talks of himself as the regenerator, the completely equipped & powerful machine. Says outright, 'If I had been in control during the war, things might have gone very differently.' Wigram & the rest frightened. Anything may happen at any moment. Here in England we havent even bought our gas masks. Nobody takes it seriously. But having seen this mad dog, the thin rigid Englishmen are really afraid. And if we have only nice public schoolboys like W. to guide us, there is some reason I suppose to expect that Oxford Street will be flooded with poison gas one of these days. And what then? Germany will get her colonies."

May 9, 1935. While they are traveling by motorcar through Germany, on their way to Italy, Leonard and Virginia Woolf are forced to make a detour as Goering has to pass with his entourage. Virginia notes: "People gathering in the sunshine—rather forced like school sports. Banners stretched across the street 'The Jew is our enemy' 'There is no place for Jews in—.' So we whizzed along until we got out of range of the docile hysterical crowd. Our obsequiousness gradually turning to anger. Nerves rather frayed. A sense of stupid mass feeling masked by good temper. So we came here, Unkel, an old country house, with curved bannister, shallow steps, a black grated stair door, & courtyard. A number of little eyes in the roof, rabbits & doves in outhouses. The innkeeper is playing cards with his wife. They all want to go away—back to Islington, back to Washington—Oh so lovely, said the waiter, who wants to go on talking."

June 1935. Between 1935 and 1941, Ernst Jünger and Carl Schmitt addressed each other in their correspondence as "Dear Herr Counselor of State!" and "Dear Herr Jünger!" They then moved on to "Dear Carl Schmitt" and "Dear Ernst Jünger." They often recommended writers and books to each other. To Schmitt, Jünger recommended *The Other Side* by Alfred Kubin: "I would much recommend you to read this. After Hoffmann, it is the best fantasy novel, with astonishing connections with our own age; one reads it as though one were passing through the cellars on which our own buildings were constructed." Schmitt followed his advice and read the book "with great excitement" while traveling in Italy.

July 22–23, 1935. Céline is in a hotel at Badgastein with two of his lovers, Lucienne Delforge and Cillie Ambor. Lucienne is a pianist and takes lessons with a concert pianist. Cillie has joined them from Vienna. The two women go trekking in the mountains. Céline is bored, exasperated. The "regularity of life" in a hotel in the Alpine foothills is not for him. Over these days Céline also continued his correspondence with Élie Faure, increasingly acrimonious, increasingly intractable. And this was his chance to say what he thought of people: "Dear Élie, the misfortune in all this is *that there is not a 'people'* in the touching sense in which you intend it, there are only exploiters and exploited, and everyone *exploited* asks only to become *exploiter*. He understands nothing else. The egalitarian heroic proletariat *doesn't exist*. It's a *vacuous dream*, a NONSENSE, hence the uselessness, the absolute, nauseating stupidity of all those ridiculous little images, the proletarian in blue overalls, the hero of tomorrow, and the nasty puffed up capitalist with his gold chain. Both of them are muck." And Céline also added a note at the end that touches on the essence of literature: "You have to give yourself entirely to the thing in itself, not to the people nor to Crédit Lyonnais, to no one."

September 1936. Samuel Beckett, age thirty, angular, depressed, decides he will spend a few months in Germany since he wants to see certain paintings, particularly the early masters—and, at the end of the list, something new, Ernst Kirchner or Erich Heckel or Emil Nolde, if anyone still dared to exhibit them. By December he had been through Hamburg, Lübeck, Lüneburg, Hannover, Braunschweig, Riddagshausen, Wolfenbüttel, Hildesheim, before settling in Berlin, where he noted: "The trip is being a failure. Germany is horrible. Money is scarce. I am tired all the time. All the modern pictures are in the cellars." At Lüneburg, he wanted to see the heath, but was disappointed ("a voice was telling me: It's the Lüneburg heath that you need"). But it didn't go like that: "I didn't like the Lüneburg heath, not at all. I went away disappointed, and at the same time relieved." At Hannover he wanted to see Leibniz's house. And in a letter written in excellent German he recounted how "Hannover was overcome by such widespread cultural enthusiasm that it could be felt even in Café Kröpcke, for the skeleton of Leibniz kept in the Neustädter Kirche had just been confirmed as authentic after a careful examination of its right big toe."

The journey followed an orderly itinerary, from north to south, from Hamburg to Munich, pursued tenaciously, with no detours, until he was overcome by a sense of weariness and surfeit ("I am tired and have had enough and can see nothing more but only look"). So Augsburg, Ulm, Stuttgart, Karlsruhe, Freiburg, Colmar, Strasburg, Frankfurt, all part of his itinerary, were lost. Meanwhile six months passed.

Beckett spent most of the time in museums. Otherwise, meetings with Germans who often belonged to the category of *friends of Rilke* ("every second person of a certain degree of culture in German seems to have been a friend of Rilke"); or with White Russians who spoke about Andrei Bely ("Biely [*sic*] and vodka go well together I found"). Although in Munich there was "nothing to go to in the evening," Beckett didn't lose a chance to see "the legend Valentin" and found him "a comedian of the very first order."

Beckett travels in Germany as many German tourists had done in nineteenth-century Italy. He clutches his Baedeker—and is not prepared to miss a thing. Not just museums and churches, but places of the Great Spirits. He visits the houses of Friedrich Klopstock, of Gotthold Lessing, Voltaire's room at Sanssouci. And politics? Very few mentions in his letters. Most of the space was taken up by the early masters and by the vicissitudes of *Murphy*, which in those months was regularly being rejected by publishers, in Britain and America. Beckett noted in passing that Thomas Mann's passport had been withdrawn; that someone was raging against the government; that a gallery owner dared to exhibit pictures by degenerate painters such as Franz Marc and Emil Nolde; that a "little German pedant" by the name of Fräulein Tiedtke insisted on writing a thesis on Proust ("there is something magnificent in doing a doctorate in 1936 with a work on not merely an 'exquisite,' but a non-Aryan").

A detailed digression on the history of Nuremberg, from the times of Dürer to those in which Beckett is writing: "They drove out the Jews in 1499 and kept them out for 3 and a half centuries. [. . .] And now it is the industrial centre of Bavaria and with Munich & Berlin the third centre of Nazidiffusion and the seat of Jewbaiting Streicher & his rag."

September 10, 1936. Roberto Bazlen writes a long letter from Milan to his friend Ludovico Sain, interspersing each sentence with words of German. He describes a short trip to Longone, north of Milan, "sehr schoen, and minimally that Brianza green of gottverlassene plain that you cannot bear and I idem. Much in ganz richtigen Waeldern, and given that Gadda was fast immer at Milan I had the most herrlichste Ruhe, and each morning I could eat a fine raw onion, was ich sehr notwendig hatte, without jemanden anzustinken." Having avoided stinking out Carlo Emilio Gadda with his raw onion, Bazlen goes on to give particular news about various friends in Trieste. Followed by details about money. And last: "Do read the most beautiful book to be published in recent years: Picard, Die Flucht vor Gott (Eugen Rentsch Verlag, Erlenbach-Zürich und Leipzig)."

In Picard's book there is a description applicable in every detail to the Islamic suicide-killers who would appear some seventy years later: "There is someone who tries to be more wicked than he is: he is fearful of not being aware of evil or even of himself, unless he commits a truly great evil. He parades evil like a banner on which is written that his home is here, he reads it himself otherwise he wouldn't know it, and others read it who run away with him, as if among those who run away it were conventionally established that this evil is valid only as a sign: here *is* someone, here there is certainly someone, here at this limit of evil there is certainly a man, for an instant one can pause beside him, he himself can pause beside himself, on the solid edge of evil."

November 28, 1936. At the Société française de Philosophie, Élie Halévy reads a communication titled "The Era of Tyrannies." Clear, very clear ideas. Mixed reactions: "The discussion was complicated for various reasons to do with the current situation, which Halévy himself had imprudently put together in the same discussion," notes Aldo Garosci, who was present at the meeting. The imprudence is evident already in the underlying argument: "The era of tyrannies dates from August 1914, in other words from the moment when the warring nations adopted a regime that can be defined in the following manner: a) From the economic point of view, vast scale nationalization of all means of production, distribution and exchange;—and, conversely, appeal by governments to the leaders of workers' organizations to assist them in this task of nationalization— hence trade unionism, corporatism, and at the same time government activism; b) From the intellectual point of view, the nationalization of thought, which takes two forms: a negative one, through the suppression of all the expressions of an opinion held contrary to the national interest; the other positive, through what we will call the organization of enthusiasm."

After the meeting, there were various reactions, mostly

hostile. But there was also a letter from Marcel Mauss. Which couldn't have been clearer: "Your deduction about the two Italian and German tyrannies starting from Bolshevism is absolutely correct, but allow me to point out two other features that you did not mention perhaps for reasons of space.

"The fundamental doctrine from which all this is deduced is that of 'active minorities,' such as one could find in the trade union–anarchist circles of Paris, and as it was elaborated in particular by Sorel, when I left 'Le Mouvement Socialiste' so as not to be a part of its campaign. A doctrine of the minority, a doctrine of violence, and even corporatism, have each spread before my eyes, from Sorel to Lenin to Mussolini. [. . .]

"Austrian Christian-social corporatism, which became that of Hitler, is originally of another order; but in the end, by copying Mussolini, it became of the same order.

"But here is the second point.

"I insist more than you on the fundamental fact of secrecy and conspiracy. I have much experience of the active circles of the P.S.R. [Socialist Revolutionary Party], etc., Russians; I followed the social democrats less well, but I knew the Bolsheviks of the Parc Montsouris and, finally, I had some experience of them in Russia. The active minority was a reality over there; it was a perpetual conspiracy. This conspiracy lasted throughout the war, throughout the Kerensky government, and won. But the formation of the Communist party remained that of a secret sect, and its essential organism, the GPU, remained the assault organization of a secret organization. The Communist party itself remains encamped in the midst of Russia, just as the Fascist party and as Hitler's party are encamped, without artillery and without fleet, but with the whole policing apparatus.

"Here I easily recognize certain events as they often happened in Greece, and which Aristotle describes very well, but which, above all, are characteristic of archaic societies and perhaps of the whole world. It is the 'Society of Men,' with its brotherhoods that are public and secret at the same time, and, in the society of men, it is the society of youth that acts.

"Sociologically it is perhaps a necessary form of action, but it is a backward form. Yet this is no reason why it shouldn't be fashionable. It satisfies the needs of secrecy, of influence, of action, of youth and often of tradition. I would add that, on the manner in which tyranny is usually linked to war and democracy itself, the pages of Aristotle can still be quoted impeccably. We seem to have returned to the days when the young men of Megara swore in secret not to stop until they had destroyed the famous constitution. Here there are repetitions, following identical patterns."

On that November day, Halévy had shown himself *imprudent* for more than one reason. First, his communication was constructed as a theorem: stated and proven. And this with an almost hallucinatory effect because, as Léon Brunschvicg observed at the beginning of the discussion, that session followed point by point another session of thirty-four years before, in which Élie Halévy had argued with Georges Sorel over the question of historical materialism. But Halévy's communication could now easily "degenerate into political argument," as Brunschvicg, president of the society, had already feared before the meeting opened. It was obvious that Halévy's ideas, too clear and too distinct, would end up touching on the current political situation in a way that, for opposite reasons, would be generally rejected. And never as much as for the final paragraph: "The Russian Revolution, born from a movement of revolt against the war, was consolidated, organized, under the form of a 'communism of war' during the two years of war with the allied armies that went from the peace of Brest-Litovsk to the final victory of the Communist armies in 1920. A new feature is added here to those that we have already described. Because of the collapse of anarchy, of the total disappearance of the State, a group of armed men, inspired by a common faith, decreed that it was itself the State: Sovietism, in such form, is a 'fascism' to the letter."

Without needing to resort to ponderous theories on totalitarianism—and without even having to use the word—Halévy had identified, in his short communication, the two features that perfectly linked what was going on in Russia, in Germany, and in Italy. First of all the presence of "active minorities" (Mauss's formula) installed within a party, which becomes the ultimate aspiration and the sole effective player (the state, at this point, was only a cover). They could call themselves "revolutionary avant-gardes" or "political combat groups" or SS and SA. In any event they were the place where decisions were effectively made, for which there was no accountability to anyone. The second feature was what Halévy described with unintentionally ironic brevity as "the organization of enthusiasm": words that were enough to evoke, in the same instant, as though in a flash, the ceremonies in the Nuremberg stadium, the parades in Red Square, and the Foro Italico, as well as posters displaying the male and female variants of the "new man," along with pictures and frescoes of Sepp Hilz, Aleksandr Deineka, and Mario Sironi. A clarity such as that shown by Halévy, a clarity simultaneous to the events discussed and free from pathos (even in Élie one noted the *dry humor* of the Halévy clan that reverberated in operetta as in the wit of Oriane de Guermantes), was bound to be disturbing.

Halévy, with his attention to detail, certainly couldn't be accused of linking together discordant facts, even if he had identified what *held together* Russia, Germany, and Italy in those years. But, in the discussion at the Société de Philosophie, he anticipated the objection that would inevitably arise: "I am far from disputing that, in many respects, apparent to everyone, the phenomena are antithetical. I went to Leningrad and I know Fascist Italy. Now, when one crosses the Russian border, there is the immediate sensation of leaving one world and entering another; and such a subversion of all values can be seen, if one wishes, as legitimizing an extreme tyranny. But, in Italy, nothing of the kind; and the traveler finds himself wondering whether there was any need for such a gigantic policing system with no other result than roads better maintained and trains more punctual."

There is a clear difference between the "era of tyrannies" and "era of dictatorships"—and Halévy wanted to make this clear. Dictatorship "implies the idea of a temporary regime, which leaves intact, in the long run, a regime of freedom." Whereas tyranny is "a normal form of government, which the scientific observer of society must place alongside other normal forms: monarchy, aristocracy and democracy." And not just this: tyranny has a physiological connection with democracy. On this point Halévy felt comforted by Mauss's approval "without reserve," particularly on the fact that "the complementary analyses of Plato and Aristotle on the way in which there was a passage in the ancient world from democracy to tyranny, find a profound application in historical phenomena of which we are today the spectators." Here Halévy was fingering the open—and perennially open—wound of democracy: the fact that Hitler was appointed chancellor by legal means. And was confirmed soon after by elections with a 90 percent turnout—a number yearned for by all advocates of a real democracy. But the question was not touched in the discussion that followed Halévy's communication. At the end of which the ill feeling among various members about the supposed "resemblance of Soviet dictatorship to Fascist and Hitlerian dictatorships" seemed increasingly apparent. In his reply, Halévy showed he could well differentiate what was happening in the three countries in question. But this did not prevent him giving a definition, incisive and hard to better, of what those regimes had in common: "As to the form (and I think everyone has accepted the point), the regimes are identical. It is the government of a country by means of an armed sect, which is imposed in the name of the supposed interest of the whole country, and which has the strength to assert itself because it feels animated by a common faith."

January 16, 1937. Martin du Gard meets Paul Léautaud in the offices of the *Mercure de France*. "They smell musty, of dusty paperwork, of old posters for auction sales, exactly the smell of a notary's office." These rooms, for Léautaud, are a second home. They talk about Gide, whom Léautaud has just seen. Léautaud: "Fool! an aging child! No! Aye! Aye! Do you remember what he had written before his trip to the USSR? He wanted to give his life for the USSR. And after he had been there, he was very annoyed. This is what it means not to have one essential quality: suspicion. A successful writer, but as for intelligence, reason: none. I've always thought so. Giving his life for the USSR, what folly! Of all his follies, this is the most remarkable."

September 6–13, 1937. Robert Brasillach had been to Mussolini's Italy. He had seen the civil war in Spain. At last it was Germany's turn. Editor of *Je Suis Partout*, a magazine brazenly favorable to "Hitlerism" (as it was then labeled), he was bound to be a most welcome guest at the Nuremburg party congress. He left with a small group of friends. They were roused by curiosity and fervor, and set off across Germany "singing 'La Madelon' under the respectful eyes of the Bavarians." It was the start of *Cent heures chez Hitler*, as Brasillach titled his on-the-spot report, published in the *Revue Universelle*.

At the outset, caution and truisms: "Neither Germany nor Hitlerism are simple matters." Certainly, it's "a strange country," it isn't easy to forget it was once enemy number one. And those small towns now come into sight, those villages that seem arranged "in the midst of delightful green landscapes, like children's toys and decorations." There are no political posters, unlike Fascist Italy. Just a large number of flags. Some, immense, cover five-story buildings. And do not clash with the old stonemasonry. "It is old Germany of the Holy Empire married with the Third Reich." The union is prepared. And people are ready to take part in the "sacred rites of the new Germany."

All is dressed up for celebration. Few words are proffered: invitations to come back next year and sometimes, as they arrive at certain villages and certain inns, the inscription "Jews are not *appreciated* here." An approach of "restrained politeness," comments Brasillach.

Having reached Nuremberg, his small group visits the great anti-Marxist exhibition. France appears through Rousseau, instigator of the Revolution. But balanced by Voltaire and Napoleon, whose "anti-Semitic phrases are set out in block capitals." More amusing, at Erlangen, was the anti-Masonic exhibition, in a lodge transformed into an educational museum. Visits with a guide. But the group is impatient. It wants to reach the "magical enclosure" in which the "Hitlerian ceremony" will take place. At last they see the outline of the Zeppelinfeld Stadium, "in that almost Mycenaean architecture so dear to the Third Reich." A hundred thousand seated, "two or three hundred thousand in the arena." Banners with the swastika glint in the sun. The work battalions file past, eighteen abreast, with spades on their shoulders:

"The workers' mass begins.

" 'Are you ready to make the German soil fertile?'

" 'We are ready.'

"They sing, the drum rolls, the dead are invoked."

Brasillach already feels close to what he was looking for: "As the stadium empties slowly of its officiants and its spectators, we have started to understand what is the new Germany."

It will become even clearer the following day. It is night. "The immense stadium is sparsely lit with a few searchlights that allow glimpses of the massive stationary battalions of the SA dressed in brown." In the middle, a corridor from the stadium entrance to the tribune of the Führer. Who arrives at precisely eight o'clock. Thunderous applause; "those who shout loudest are the Austrians." Innumerable searchlights are suddenly switched on, pointing to the sky. "There are a thousand blue pillars that now encircle it, like a mysterious cage."

Then silence. One single spotlight on the "red mass" of flags that move toward the platform like "a flow of purple lava." Twenty minutes of "supernatural and mineral silence." Brasillach, a man of the cinema, notes: "I don't believe I have seen such a magnificent spectacle in my life." At last even Cecil B. DeMille might discover what is truly "the greatest spectacle on earth."

Dinner at the gates of Nuremberg, "at the camp of the SS. We will be received by Monsieur Himmler, chief of the SS, leader of the Gestapo, and Monsieur Goebbels in person will preside over the dinner." An official banquet like many others, with sauerkraut, Bavarian sausage, dry Franconian wine. But at the end there is the moment of silence when the flag is lowered. A trumpet "sounded a nostalgic air, and slowly the red flag with swastika came down." It is the moment for serious, solemn thoughts. And Brasillach asks whether "great feelings are now incomprehensible for France." He thinks, painfully, "about what democracy has done for France."

And Hitler? Brasillach had already heard him in 1933, on the radio and at the cinema. Now he gives the impression of "a greater moderation. He no longer gesticulates, he speaks almost non-stop with his hands folded." Brasillach and his friends are invited by von Ribbentrop to a tea where Hitler's arrival is expected. At last he appears: "The usual uniform, which is surprising, the yellowish jacket, black trousers. The tuft. A tired face. Even more sad than one imagined. Only up close does one see his smile. An almost childish smile, as leaders so often have. 'He is so nice,' his collaborators say in a surprising way. Several people are presented to him, he shakes hands with an absent look, responds with few words. And we remain there, stunned." There is something else: his eyes. "They are eyes of another world, strange eyes, deep blue and black, in which the pupil can barely be distinguished. How can one guess what is going on in them?" Perhaps "a boundless love for *Deutschland*, the German land, that land that is real and has still to be built"? But one thing is certain: "Those eyes are grave. Filled with an almost insurmountable anguish, with an unprecedented anxiety . . . We feel strongly, physically, what a terrible ordeal it is to lead a nation, to lead Germany toward its voracious destiny." Brasillach concludes: "I believe I will never forget the color and the sadness of Hitler's eyes, which are without doubt his enigma."

Thinking back, the most intense moment for him was that of the consecration of the flags: "They present to the Führer the 'blood flag,' the one carried by demonstrators killed during the failed *Putsch* of 1923. [. . .] The Chancellor took the blood flag with one hand, and with the other the new banners that he had to consecrate. Through him it could be said that an unknown fluid is passed and that the benediction of the martyrs is now extended to new symbols of the German homeland. A purely symbolic ceremony? I don't think so." For Brasillach, symbolism is not enough. There has to be "a sort of mystical transfusion similar to that of water blessed by the priest—if it is not, dare we say, that of the Eucharist. Those who do not see the analogy between the consecration of the flags and the consecration of the bread, a sort of German sacrament, run the risk of not understanding anything about Hitlerism."

Indeed, those who debated whether Hitlerism was pagan or Christian—Brasillach implied—had understood nothing. It was both. But above all it made both superfluous. It made everything superfluous, apart from itself. Pagan sacrifice? It was a timid approximation of what the chancellor was offering: "He would sacrifice everything, human happiness, even his own and that of his people, if required by the mysterious duty that he obeyed." And there

is no doubt that this "mysterious duty" is continually re-
quiring it. And Christian sacrifice? It is repeated at each
consecration of the flags. And so fairly often. And with
traces of true blood. It is no coincidence that Brasillach has
written "transfusion" and not "transubstantiation." There
is no more mention of a "memorial." Symbols are no longer needed. Wine is no longer transformed into blood.
There is congealed blood that now flows in the blood of
the living.

Brasillach himself is rather frightened by what he is saying: "It is at this point that we are anxious." But he raises
no objections. And leaves Nuremberg with this "final impression . . . fine spectacles, fine youth, life easier than what
people say, but above all the surprising mythology of a
new religion." Slimy, rancid politics are at an end. People are now talking of *mythology* and *religion*. Invented,
founded, and put into practice in four years. Ready to be
extended everywhere, with beneficial effects. Brasillach,
the man who had made his debut with a book on Virgil,
who had pulled Nonnus and Lycophron out of some rarely
visited bookshelves of the École Normale library, who had
conversed brilliantly with Valéry, Giraudoux, and Thibaudet, who had been kindly looked upon by Colette, who
worshipped Tintoretto and Carpaccio, who had written
about Hollywood in one of the first histories of cinema,
returned to Paris with these firm convictions, after his
"hundred hours" at Hitler's Nuremberg.

1939. Not everyone wanted to read the 778 pages of
Mein Kampf. But quite a few swooped on *Hitler m'a dit* by

Hermann Rauschning, which appeared then for the first time in Paris. After all, it wasn't the work of a mere journalist, but of someone who had been president of the Senate in the free city of Danzig in 1933–1934. And there was no doubt he had seen Hitler from close up.

Only toward the end of the book does Rauschning reveal Hitler's esoteric doctrine: "I will tell you a secret. I am founding an Order." Something similar to the Teutonic Order of Knights. A small number had already met at Marienburg Castle. But Hitler saw a future for the order constellated with castles: "In my *Ordensburgen* a youth will grow up before which the world will shrink back. [. . .] One thing they must learn—self-command! They shall learn to overcome the fear of death, under the severest tests. That is the intrepid and heroic stage of youth. Out of it comes the stage of the free man, the man who is the substance and essence of the world, the creative man, the godman. In my *Ordensburgen* there will stand as a statue for worship the figure of the magnificent, self-ordaining godman; it will prepare the young men for their coming period of ripe manhood."

And the Jews? Hitler had spoken earlier about them, for the Jews were also part of his "esoteric doctrine," which "implies an almost metaphysical antagonism to the Jew." But Rauschning wanted to know more: "I asked whether that amounted to saying that the Jew must be destroyed.

"'No,' he replied. 'We should then have to invent him. It is essential to have a tangible enemy, not merely an abstract one.'"

April 18, 1939. As Ernst Jünger is digging footpaths for his garden at Kirchhorst, he realizes his spade "is cutting worms to pieces, which twist and writhe. In these images the pain briefly touches us like a cauterizing tip. We understand that the pain is symbolized in the worm and that when man suffers without defense he can be compared to the worm. Meanwhile, there is the position, at ground level, image of baseness, without having the rapidity of the snake, its armor and its weaponry. And then there is that bare skin, with no hair or protection, blindness and above all that writhing through which the whole body becomes a mirror of sensation.

"Whenever we see a worm writhing, repugnance is blended with pity, as with the pig, which it resembles in the way it suffers. I suppose they both live out their existence without a care: the worm lives in the rich soil as in a Land of Cockaigne and the pig lets itself fall to the rank of voracious eater, which presupposes, if not an acquiescence, at least a predisposition. On the other hand, there are animals that are seen to suffer very nobly."

But pigs and worms stir a further meditation. What do they have in common? Might it not be the case to observe that "atrocities easily affect certain types that have a particular relationship with the crude and physical substance of pain"? But of what will this family of beings consist, this family no less "mysterious" than that of worms? For example, of certain "women who openly arouse lust," or of certain people who are "obsessed by the desire for a comfortable, opulent life." These are the type of beings who attract atrocities: "For example, those in great danger are the ones people call bloodsuckers, and loose women attract butchers." It couldn't be clearer. "Pigs" and "worms" were epithets applied (already for a long time) to Jews. Though they could in the end refer to others. But "bloodsuckers"? That was the word reserved specifically for Jews, inasmuch as they sucked the healthy blood of the people. The war had yet to begin, but in his digressions as a gardener and naturalist Jünger had already gleaned what was about to happen. "Naked fear always attracts the terrible."

June 7, 1939. In the postscript of a letter to Margarete Steffin, Walter Benjamin writes: "Karl Kraus has died too soon. Listen to this: the Vienna Gas Company has stopped supplying gas to Jews. The consumption of gas by the Jewish population brought losses for the Gas Company, because despite being the biggest consumers they did not pay their bills. The Jews preferred to use the gas for the purpose of suicide."

August 23, 1939. Arthur Koestler is reading the Havas news agency report in the *Eclaireur du Sud-Est* about the Hitler-Stalin pact and starts beating his temples with his fists. Daphne Hardy is standing beside him. "Stalin has joined Hitler," he tells her. "He would," she replies. She was twenty-three, "was born in the year of the Treaty of Versailles and could not understand why a man of thirty-five should make such a fuss at the funeral of his illusions—belonging, as she did, to a generation with none."

They were living happily then in what was left of the villa of an anglophile lover of the prince of Monaco, "la Perle de la Vésubie," at Roquebillière, inland from the Côte d'Azur. Koestler was writing *Darkness at Noon* and he had only just put the following words into the mouth of his character Gletkin, the NKVD inquisitor: "We did not recoil from betraying our friends and compromising with our enemies, in order to preserve the Bastion. That was the task which history has given us, the representatives of the first victorious revolution."

Koestler recounted those days in *Scum of the Earth*, written between January and March 1941, before the German attack on Russia. At that moment, the pact signed by Molotov and von Ribbentrop became a sinister memory. And the USSR could seem like the final bastion. But Koestler didn't want to change a word of the account of his reactions to news of the pact and, in his author's note of August 1941, he added an illuminating sentence, which reverberates over everything written about those years, *after* those years: "To smuggle in elements of a later knowledge when describing the mental pattern of people in an earlier period is a common temptation to writers, which should be resisted."

And so this, for him and for Daphne, was their experience of the beginning of the war. They had stopped at Le Lavandou, at the Restaurant des Pêcheurs, "one of those enchanting little inns which make one remember meals in France like gaily-colored landmarks of the past." At a certain point "the waitress came in with the *entrecôte*, and said in a flat voice, while arranging dishes on the table: 'They have just announced on the wireless that early this morning the Germans opened fire on Poland. The Government has decreed general mobilization.'" But more than the words, at that moment it was the effect of the scene: "There was only an old couple in the restaurant apart from us, sitting at a neighboring table. They were both in black, and the woman, with protruding, red-veined eyes, nodded to us in mournful reproach. She had eaten and drunken an enormous amount without losing her mournful look—the type of Frenchwoman who already as a bride has the future widow written on her face. She went on nodding at us in silence, and it seemed to me that with her appraising eyes she tried to divine what G. [Daphne Hardy] would look like with a black veil. One felt that a great time began for her now, a sort of Indian summer blooming, nourished by the black saps of general despair."

June 10, 1940. Giaime Pintor is twenty-one years old, translates from Rilke, and has also been practicing his German on the *Völkischer Beobachter*. With two friends— Mischa Kamenetzky, who later changes his name to Ugo Stille and sails for America to escape the racial persecutions, and Valentino Gerratana, a future official of the Italian Communist Party—he joins "the flood of people on their way to Piazza Venezia. An enormous crowd occupied the square; we were squashed into a corner among those curious people of Rome who quarrel and laugh in the most serious of situations. After much clamoring and calling, the doors opened and Mussolini appeared. I heard almost nothing of the speech; we were in a point where we couldn't hear. 'What's he said?' asked those nearby when a roar of enthusiasm interrupted the Duce. Then came the words 'ambassadors of France and England,' 'delivered' . . . and the three of us realized it was war. Until that moment no one was sure. The speech was brief and then all those rowdy and delighted people poured into the streets and ran to the Quirinal Palace to hail the King. Bewildered, we followed the movement of the crowd, looking at the excited faces of the women and enjoying the splendid June twilight."

June 1940. Klaus Mann in New York, appalled by the news: "The Nazis in Paris. Germany jubilant, even the 'other' Germany. Hitler throws himself into dances of joy." A few days later, the most shocking thought: "If Hitler were to march on London as on Paris, without America moving a finger, what would become of American democracy? An America that tolerates the victory of fascism would itself be ripe for fascism. A terrible thought! In place of a senile marshal, the Quisling role would be taken by the handsome transatlantic pilot. Charles Lindbergh at the White House . . ." A few days later, the appearance of "a strange new acquaintance: the young Carson McCullers, author of the fine novel *The Heart Is a Lonely Hunter*. She has just arrived from the South. A curious mixture of refinement and wildness, 'morbidezza' and naivety. Perhaps very gifted. The work she is involved in at the moment should be about a negro and a Jewish emigrant: two outcasts. Something interesting could come out of it."

Autumn 1940. Lisbon has become "the bottleneck of Europe." All those under persecution are passing through. More or less everyone, "from A, for Austrian Monarchist, to Z, for Zionist Jew. Every European nation, religion, party was represented in that procession, including German Nazis of Strasser's oppositional faction and Italian Fascists in disgrace." Koestler watches them. He is one of them, one of the many. Indeed, he belongs to several of those categories. As a last resort, he had enlisted in the Foreign Legion under the name Albert Dubert ("I thought 'Dubert' sounded very respectable indeed: it was the name of the chief of police of Limoges").

There is a constant arrival of news about arrests, disappearances, suicides. Above all, suicides. This was worrying the French authorities: "A considerable portion of the German political exiles were still in concentration camps, such as Le Vernet, or imprisoned for the second and third times, waiting for their extradition to Germany on the strength of paragraph 19 of the Armistice Treaty. As the number of suicides increased, special precautions were taken by the French authorities." The reason was that "the merchandise had to be kept ready for delivery."

But news of suicides continued to flow in—and Koestler noted: "And more suicides: Otto Pohl, Socialist veteran, Austrian ex-Consul in Moscow, ex-Editor of the 'Moskauer Rundschau.' Walter Benjamin, author and critic, my neighbor in 10, rue Dombasle in Paris, fourth at our Saturday poker parties, and one of the most bizarre and witty persons I have known. Last time I had met him was in Marseilles, together with H., the day before my departure, and he had asked me: 'If anything goes wrong, have you got anything to take?' For in those days we all carried some 'stuff' in our pockets like conspirators in a penny dreadful; only reality was more dreadful. I had none, and he shared what he had with me, sixty-two tablets of a sedative, procured in Berlin during the week which followed the burning of the Reichstag. He did it reluctantly, for he did not know whether the thirty-one tablets left him would be enough. It was enough. A week after my departure he made his way over the Pyrenees to Spain, a man of fifty-five, with heart disease. At Port Bou, the *Guardia Civil* arrested him. He was told that next morning they would send him back to France. When they came to fetch him for the train, he was dead."

1941. Simone Weil is struck by a collection of recently published writings by Max Planck. She sees in Planck, much more than in Einstein, the person who has caused a "radical break in the development of science." The idea of quanta is "extraordinary and subversive in itself," even if perhaps it is wrong, in some of its applications. But it will become the new foundation of the world. There is then a strange fact: as soon as Planck moves away from quanta, everything he says is banal. He speaks like a decent man "in the ordinary meaning of the word," possessed of good sense, "which is already much." But no more. So the world is said to be based on a science it cannot understand, discovered by a man who, beyond science, has nothing meaningful to say. And yet it is "in the name of science that we, white people [. . .] walk the terrestrial globe as its masters, treading, at every step, on some treasure." Science is for Westerners what the Catholic Church was for Cortés and Pizarro. Except that these still had some idea about what the sacraments were.

Two years later, in London, Simone Weil wrote the *Prelude to a Declaration of Duties Toward Mankind*. She wanted to single out some unshakable principles. And she questioned what to rely on. Religion was no longer of use, as it was now something "for Sunday morning." And science? Only nonbelievers, who yet believe in everyday science, "have a triumphant feeling of inner unity." A feeling that is illusory, however. Their morality is "in contradiction with science no less than the religion of others." Science, in fact, is not moral. Inasmuch as no rules of behavior are offered. Weil reaches these conclusions: "Hitler has seen it clearly. What's more, he lets many people see it, wherever there is the presence or menace of the SS, and even further away. Today only unreserved adherence to a totalitarian system, brown, red or other, can give, so to speak, a solid illusion of inner unity. This is why it constitutes such a strong temptation for so many souls in disarray."

January 12, 1941. André Gide, a far less expert gardener than Jünger, also dwelt on horticultural imaginings, especially when dealing with moments of the greatest pain. He took his inspiration from far away, talking to himself: "Have you noticed, at times when you were busy gardening, that the only way for preserving, protecting and safeguarding what is exquisite, what is best, was to suppress what is less good? You know that this cannot happen without giving an impression of cruelty, but that this cruelty is prudence." What is Gide talking about? Certainly not about himself, being much more urban than rural. He is talking about Hitler, "who wants to be the great gardener of Europe." Perhaps no one, until then, had ventured to describe him as such. But in Paris one always finds something more subtle, more polished than anywhere else.

Yet Gide is also the man of doubt and of constant self-revision. How then is the enterprise of that new European gardener to be described? "That work is not so much superhuman as inhuman." It has to be asked whether "that which his force destroys doesn't have a greater value, infinitely, than that force itself and what it claims to offer us." His punch is hard and unexpected—and requires a momentary pause. But he immediately resumes: "Your dream is great, Hitler; but the cost of achieving it is too high." It is a passage of an intimacy far greater than that displayed between Goethe and Napoleon. And immediately the sad conclusion, with regard to that dream: "If it fails (since it is too superhuman to be achieved), what will there remain on earth, at the end of it all, apart from grief and devastation?"

February–March 1941. Princess Marie—"Missie" to her friends—Vassiltchikov (White Russian, aged twenty-four, beautiful) was working happily at the Information Department of the Ministry of Foreign Affairs in Berlin. "The atmosphere there is much more congenial," she noted, thinking of her previous job with the Radio Service, employed by Goebbels. The offices had been "fully equipped with bathrooms, kitchens, etc." A privilege in time of war. And above all, Missie would almost invariably speak English with her boss Adam von Trott zu Solz and other officials. One of these, "a very nice man respected by all," is replaced by a "young and aggressive S.S. Brigadier by the name of Stahlecker, who strides around in high boots, swinging a whip, a German shepherd dog at his side. Everyone is worried by this change." They avoid Stahlecker as much as they can. "There is something sinister about him."

But Stahlecker would remain at the ministry for only a short time. In June he is appointed head of the Einsatzgruppe A, the task force operating in the Baltic states and in Belorussia. In a report to Berlin of winter 1941, Stahlecker writes that Einsatzgruppe A had already killed 249,420 Jews.

June 1941. Peter Viereck was twenty-four and had graduated *summa cum laude* at Harvard University. His main worry was his father. George Sylvester Viereck was the author of books that included a vampire novel, promoter of a hormone rejuvenation treatment, and one of the first American reporters to interview Hitler, in 1923. He had found him to be "a widely read, thoughtful" man. George Sylvester was eventually known as George Swastika Viereck since he promoted Nazism (though purged of its anti-Semitism). The FBI eventually arrested him for conspiracy.

Young Viereck looked around and realized that Americans knew little, and understood even less, about Hitler. Many thought that Hitler had invented his ideas—or in any event that his ideas didn't much matter. So Viereck set about writing *Metapolitics*, which appeared just before Pearl Harbor. With enthusiasm and vigor he tried to reconstruct the path "From the Romantics to Hitler" (this was the subtitle), demonstrating that some of Hitler's ideas had been immensely popular in low, medium, and high culture in nineteenth-century Germany.

During those same months Bertolt Brecht was writing *The Resistible Rise of Arturo Ui*, where Hitler is presented as a gangster trying to take control of the cauliflower racket. Young Viereck couldn't know it, but in the introduction to *Metapolitics* he was already perfectly reiterating Brecht and many who would follow him: "The common question is: are the men on top, Hitler particularly, as sincere as the masses below or only cynical gangsters laughing at their own stolen ideas? But the very question is too heavy-footed, too lacking in psychological awareness, to answer either positively or negatively. Here the real question is not either-or. Both the 'either' and the 'or' combine; that combination is a logical impossibility but a psychological fact. In other words, most successful frauds are sincere; most demagogues are honestly intoxicated by their own dishonest and cynical appeals."

June 18, 1941. Curzio Malaparte is by the Black Sea, "on the threshold of the U.S.S.R." At the other end of the bridge over the Brateș "rises the Soviet triumphal arch, a rustic structure surmounted by the ritual trophy of the hammer and sickle." But on this side? "A crowd of Greeks, Armenians, gypsies, Turks and Jews swarm in a cloud of yellow dust, in a tumult of raucous voices, of yells, of laughter, of shrieks, of songs blaring from gramophones. And pervading everything is that smell of horses' urine and attar of rose which is the smell of the Levant, the smell of the Black Sea.

"The pavements of every street are flanked by hundreds and hundreds of cafés, haberdashers' shops, perfumeries, barbers' saloons, *croitoris'* window-displays, confectioners' shops, dentists' surgeries. The Greek barbers with their olive complexions, their enormous black eyebrows and their huge black moustaches glistening with brilliantine; the women's *coiffeurs*, their thick jet-black hair curled with hot irons and arranged in baroque styles; the Turkish pastry cooks, their hands dripping with honey and butter, their arms plastered up to the elbows with grated almonds and pistachio-dust; the perfumers, shoemakers, photographers, tailors, tobacconists and dentists—all greet you in sing-song voices, with solemn gestures and deep bows. All invite you to come in, to sit down, to try a comb, a razor, a suit of clothes, a pair of shoes, a hat, a truss, a pair of spectacles, a set of false teeth, a bottle of perfume, or else to have your hair curled, cut or dyed. And all the while the Turkish coffee foams in the little pots of gleaming copper, and the newsvendors shout the headlines of the *Actiunea* or recite in loud voices the latest *communiqués* on the '*situatia pe fronturile del lupta*,' and interminable processions of hairy, painted, curly-headed women pass to and fro along the pavements in front of the café tables, which are crowded with fat Levantines sitting with legs wide apart, as in the drawings of Pascin, who came from Brăila."

June 28–July 6, 1941. At Iași, in Moldavia, around 13,000 Jews were killed over little more than a week. Hitler had launched Operation Barbarossa on June 22 by sending his troops to invade Russia. On June 27, Marshall Antonescu had ordered Colonel Constantin Lupu, commandant of the garrison at Iași, to eliminate any Jewish presence. All Jews had to be regarded as crypto-Soviets, as enemies operating behind their backs. The population of Iași took part in unison, alongside German and Romanian troops, in the operation ordered by Antonescu. All sections played their part in the killings and lootings. They were united, irrespective of class or wealth.

Malaparte was "the only Italian officer in all Moldavia." The Soviets had already begun bombing. He had to find a safe shelter. Malaparte pushed open a door and went into a house that must have been hurriedly abandoned. "The window curtains had been torn down and the shreds were scattered about the rooms." The goose feathers of a ripped-open mattress whirled about the bedroom. It was "a little house at the end of a large abandoned orchard at the head of Lapusneanu Street, close to the Jockey Club and to the Café Restaurant Corso," the most elegant in the city. The abandoned orchard, as Malaparte later realized, was the old orthodox cemetery of Iași.

"A strange anguish weighed upon the city. A huge, massive and monstrous disaster, oiled, polished, tuned up like a steel machine was going to catch and grind into a pulp the houses, the trees, the streets and the inhabitants of Jassy." Malaparte had accompanied Marioara, the sixteen-year-old waitress at the Café Corso, home after the cease-fire. As they were saying good-bye, "from the Nicolina, Socola, and Pacurari districts rose a confused din, a rattle of machine guns and the dull thud of hand grenades.

" 'Oh, oh, oh, they are killing the Jews,' said Marioara holding her breath."

Malaparte then let Marioara go into her house and tried to find the street toward the orthodox cemetery: "In Unirii Square a group of SS men kneeling by the Prince Gutsa Voda monument fired their tommy guns toward the little square where the statue of Prince Ghiha in Moldavian costume stands with his great quilted coat and his brow covered by a tall fur cap. By the light of the fires a black, gesticulating throng, mostly women, could be seen huddled at the foot of the monument. From time to time someone rose, darted this way or that across the square and fell under the bullets of the SS men. Hordes of Jews pursued by soldiers and maddened civilians armed with knives and crowbars fled along the streets: groups of policemen smashed in house doors with their rifle butts; windows opened suddenly and screaming disheveled women in nightgowns appeared with their arms raised in the air; some threw themselves from windows and their faces hit the asphalt with a dull thud. Squads of soldiers hurled hand grenades through the little windows level with the street into the cellars where many people had vainly sought safety; some soldiers dropped to their knees to look at the results of the explosions within the cellars and turned laughing faces to their companions." This was just the start.

July 20, 1941. Goebbels was careful to distinguish his ministerial speeches from his journalistic articles. They were two different styles. For his speeches, a fifteen-minute dictation to the stenographer was enough. On certain days of great stress, according to Hans Schwarz van Berk, anyone in the waiting room might see the stenographer leave after twelve minutes. His articles were very different. Scrupulous preparation: documents and quotes were checked. Sometimes, according to the same Schwarz van Berk, the article could be held back for a week and "every word was weighed as if on laboratory scales." In those articles Goebbels sought to compete with the great popular journalists of those newspapers most hated by the regime, such as the *Frankfurter Zeitung*. He wanted to beat them on their own ground. Just as he wanted Germany's UFA film studio to beat Hollywood.

During the war, Goebbels published a collection of his articles with an appropriate title: *Die Zeit ohne Beispiel* (The Time Without Equal). The names of Mr. Churchill, Lord Halifax, Mr. Roosevelt, Monsieur Daladier, Mr. Chamberlain were scattered across the pages, as if the war were a matter to be settled with them. And finally it was the turn of the Jews, to whom he devoted only one article out of eighty-seven. The title was "Mimikry." And it came straight to the point: "The Jews are well known for the fact that they are masters at adapting to the environment or situation of the moment, without however losing their essence. They practice mimicry (*Mimikry*)." Revealed in just a few words was the secret of the Jews, over which so many had pondered for so many years: the talent of imitation. Which was not to be regarded as a pardonable vice, Goebbels immediately warned: "It is a system of public deception that, if applied long enough, produces a paralysis of the spirit and soul of an entire population and over time it suffocates every natural defense." And he immediately gives an example of it: if National Socialism had not appeared, "our country would have been ripe for Bolshevism, that diabolical infection which Judaism can bring upon a people." But weren't Jews above all accomplices of capitalism? "The crassest plutocracy uses socialism to reach the crassest financial dictatorship. With the help of world revolution this experiment, already carried out in the Soviet Union, had to be applied to other peoples. The result would have been Jewish world domination." What consequences were in store for the Jews? "The punishment that will be visited on them will be terrible. We can do nothing about it, it will come by itself, for it must come."

We do not know whether these words were weighed on laboratory scales. But Goebbels had certainly wanted to touch upon the crucial point: hatred for the Jews did not depend on questions of history or doctrine, but went back much further, to the time when Homo had developed his capacity for imitation to the point of assimilating himself to his earliest enemies: predators. Whereas now—suggested Goebbels—the Jews would have to compete with other men, who hadn't had to assimilate themselves to predators, because they were self-appointed primordial predators. National Socialists, unlike Jews, hadn't had to imitate anyone. They were always and only themselves. A rock-

solid, refractory, impenetrable identity. It was therefore for
them to carry out the "terrible punishment" of the Jews.
The Nazis were the belated retaliation by the animal world
against the species that had violated its order; and the Jews
were the elected representatives of that species.

Over the centuries, the most serious and shameful ac-
cusations had been heaped on the Jews: the condemnation of Jesus, foul customs, ritual killings, usury. But all this
now dissolved and a single intact and sufficient charge
remained—an offense that could even be mistaken for a
talent: *the Jew can imitate*. And the poison was concealed in
the corollary: the Jew can imitate so well as to make those
he imitates resemble him, thus succeeding, in the end, in
manipulating them. No more was needed to establish the
age-old Jewish conspiracy. Goebbels, who was a show-
man, had understood this very well: the closer the "terrible
punishment" became for the Jews, the more the accusa-
tion against them had to be reduced to its ultimate essence.
And what could be more serious than to go back to that
event, lost in the mist of prehistory? Almost everything was
a consequence of it.

July 31, 1941. The zeal of certain local populations in
killing Jews began to cause concern among several departments of the German Security Services (SD), which noted
what was happening in their reports: "The Romanians
proceed in an extremely chaotic manner with regard to
the Jews. There would be no objection against the very
many shootings of Jews if the technical preparation and

implementation were not entirely inadequate. The Romanians generally leave those executed where they are, without burying them. Operational command has urged the Romanian police to proceed more systematically in this respect."

Summer 1941. Paris area. Felix Hartlaub observes: "*Il fait lourd*. It seems like a heavy gray gas is seeping from the walls. Like someone who ought now to start catching his breath and instead continues breathing out, between his teeth, with his temples pulsating. As if something had suddenly given way in the structure of the stones, as if their pores had dilated. Place Vendôme is enveloped in a genuinely blue haze [. . .] Cultural activities: the Berlin State Opera in Paris. A prima donna abruptly raises her cadaverous white face and shows just a small part of it between her fur coat and a bouquet of flowers."

Summer 1941. Hans Carossa: "From the summer of 1941, strange rumors circulated from mouth to mouth, which at first were not believed everywhere, but then little by little were confirmed: the great fanatic had decided to kill poor little lunatics. This time I did not doubt the accuracy of what I had been told: certain arithmetic problems in our small daughter's new schoolbook had prepared me. 'One mentally ill person,' they said, 'costs the nation such-and-such an amount every year—how much do three mentally ill people cost? How much do thirty cost? etc.'"

October 7–11, 1941. He was sixty-three. He was a doctor and *Dichter*, a word only the Germans have, meaning poet, prose writer, author: someone who shapes words. He was too well known as a writer for the association of writers of the Third Reich not to keep notice of him, not to expect him to pledge his name. All that Hans Carossa had written, all that he would still be writing years later, responded always to one quality: it was even-tempered. The modulation of the sentence allowed for no abruptness. In astonishment, the reader followed that slow and unruffled buildup of words. Nothing like an even-tempered writer could attract the political and literary authorities of that moment. And above all a writer whose roots and branches were undoubtedly in the woodland of Bohemia, part of that Great Germany that was supposed to make its mark across the world from the far north to the Dardanelles.

Hans Carossa reached Weimar with the feeling that a noose was tightening around his neck. But he had seen many other *Dichter* along the way. For a moment he thought, with a hint of peasant cunning, that perhaps it was good. It would have been easier to go unnoticed. Soon he realized that even cunning can be childish. He arrived in Weimar at seven in the morning, at noon he had already been appointed president of a European Association of Writers about which he knew nothing and feared the worst. One point alone seemed certain: that for the few French-language writers that he worshipped in their immense distance—glamorous names like André Gide, Paul Claudel, Paul Valéry—there was something about the association that would make them avoid even a passing contact. He would remain alone with the *Dichters* who were swarming the streets of Weimar. The moment also came for speeches, for the closing remarks. They told him everyone was expecting a few words from him. Hans Carossa said: "There certainly is in all of you, my dear sirs, as there is in me, a firm belief that change in the West can come only from the spirit and the soul. In this conviction I accept with gratitude the expression of your trust."

October 10, 1941. Field Marshall Walter von Reichenau, commander of the German Sixth Army, issues an ordinance with precise instructions on how troops must behave as they head east. Two weeks earlier, 33,771 Jews had been shot dead by the SS or by members of combat groups—and were then left lying in the ravine at Babi Yar. Immediately after, a unit of engineers had covered them over. A few days after the field marshal's ordinance, 1,865 Jews would be killed at Lubny, near Kiev, following the same procedure. Each time they would be rounded up for a fictitious transportation and executed just outside the towns. Carried out once again by the Wehrmacht, in conjunction with the SS and the SD-Einsatzkommando (Special Combat Group) operating in the area.

Von Reichenau sought to provide a general justification for these actions that contravened military regulations. So his ordinance began with ideological considerations: "With regard to the behavior of troops toward the Bolshevik system, ideas remain that are still for various reasons not clear. The essential purpose of the campaign against the Jewish-Bolshevik system is the complete overthrow of the instruments of power and the extermination of the Asiatic influence within the European cultural circle. As a consequence, troops also have tasks that go beyond traditional and unilateral military behavior.

"The soldier in eastern regions is not only a fighter according to the rules of the art of war, but the bearer of an inexorable national-popular idea and the avenger of all the bestial acts that have been committed against the German people and those related to them. Therefore the German soldier must fully understand the necessity for a hard but just punishment of Jewish sub-humanity."

Field Marshal von Reichenau would die of an apoplectic fit in January 1942 on a flight from Poltava to Germany. Goebbels took part at his funeral, but remained dissatisfied, as he noted in his diary: "At midday the state funeral of Field Marshal von Reichenau took place. Prepared by Supreme Command, extremely poor, psychologically clumsy, with an absolutely amateurish music. After the national anthems pupils of the army music school perform the first movement of the Fifth Symphony so far as they can. I agree with General Schmundt that in future Wehrmacht state funerals be substantially entrusted to our Ministry, since only we offer the guarantee that they can be carried out in a form worthy of the State."

1942, Paris. With lovers, fixed or multiple, in German uniform: among the famous ladies of the city are Arletty, Martine Carol, Coco Chanel, Corinne Luchaire, Mireille Balin, Florence Gould, Marie-Laure de Noailles, Michèle Alfa, Madeleine de Mumm.

Arletty, mistress of the salty one-liner, says to Mireille Balin and Michèle Alfa: "We ought to start up a union." They were filming *La Femme que j'ai le plus aimée*.

Summer 1942. Felix Hartlaub was in charge of the War Diary service at the Führer's headquarters. He now found himself in Ukraine, taking notes as he observed—a practice he would follow until April 1945, when he disappeared while trying to reach an improvised unit for the defense of Berlin: "Big and white female figures descend slowly into the river along the rounded hump of granite, they hold each other by the shoulders, muffled laughter, single sonorous words over the expanse of water. But even whiter are the bras and the underpants they wear. Some heads of girls swimming out in the river, their breathing can be heard, dark wet hair falls over their broad faces. The river in some parts is smooth as if polished, elsewhere it is shaded by clumps of water plants that rise up swaying almost to the surface. Leaves of water lilies already reflect a little moonlight along the banks. Standing on the rock some soldiers are smoking, air force servicemen in their casual summer uniform—light blue-gray shirts with sleeves rolled up, short dark brown canvas shorts. The golden hairs on their knees and on their tanned arms strangely glistening. They look at the moon, they gaze at their cigarette smoke, they contemplate the shuffling tips of their shoes; they put off any attempt at launching into conversation. It would seem they have been disturbed while starting up an innocent tussle and water battle with the girl swimmers . . .

"And only now in a rocky gorge do we notice a dark

mass, enormous padded shoulders, broad caps, a thin leg of a boy that ends in a large shapeless shoe dangles over the edge of the rock and moves rhythmically: a group of village boys, the younger brothers of the girl bathers and their companions. Moving closer one feels the relentless tension of their gazes, threatening and yet inviting, which they fix on the soldiers without batting an eye. They create an area between the soldiers and the girls that is difficult to cross, and at the same time they establish a relationship."

August 30, 1942. Having arrived at Sigmaringen for the wedding of Konstantin of Bavaria, Missie Vassiltchikov was immediately taken to the castle, "perched on top of a rock in the very middle of the little town, all roofs, gables and turrets like one of those gingerbread castles in German fairy tales. We entered a lift at the bottom of the rock and were taken up about ten floors." Once in her room, Missie would like a bath and a short sleep while the guests are at Mass in the family chapel. She is offered some boiled eggs and a peach. It is hard to sleep since the organ is playing so loud. In bed, Missie reads the guest list, "which seems to include millions of Hohenzollerns and Wittelsbachs, most of them well advanced in age." Later, Konstantin takes Missie along "endless corridors, upstairs, downstairs, upstairs again," to meet the bride. Young archdukes, "slim and well-mannered," pop out from rooms along the corridors, like in a musical.

August 31, 1942. The wedding day of H.R.H. Princess Maria-Aldegunde von Hohenzollern with H.R.H. Prince

Konstantin of Bavaria, at Sigmaringen castle. This is the program:

8.15 Holy Communion in the Castle Chapel.

8.30 Breakfast in the Ancestors' Hall and King's Room.

10.00 Guests to assemble in the Green and Black Drawing-Rooms.

10.15 Procession to the town church.

10.30 Wedding ceremony and High Mass in the town church.

Following the ceremony:—congratulations:

1. Staff—King's Room
2. Officials—Ancestors' Hall
3. Invited outside guests—French Drawing-Room
4. Relatives and house guests—Green and Black Drawing-Rooms

13.30 Wedding luncheon in the Portuguese Gallery. Guests to assemble in the Green and Black Drawing-Rooms.

Dress: Gentlemen—white tie or full-dress uniform with decorations and ribbons; ladies—short dress with hat, with decorations, without ribbons.

16.30 Tea in the Old-German Hall.

17.30 The newlyweds depart by car.

The previous day saw a program no less hectic and detailed. At the end of the wedding luncheon the menus were circulated with the signatures of those present. That of Missie Vassiltchikov came back to her without having made the complete round, "scribbled all over with names such as 'Bobby,' 'Fritzi,' 'Sasha,' 'Willy,' 'Uncle Albert,' etc. And then comes, in rather childish writing, a huge solitary 'Hohenzollern.'" This was the bride's youngest brother, aged nine.

September 1, 1942. Back in Berlin, Missie Vassiltchikov thinks back over the wedding of Konstantin of Bavaria: "Since this may well be the last event of its sort until the war is over (and God knows what Europe will be like after that!) I have kept the program."

March 4, 1943. Along with the battle of Stalingrad came the end of work on *Münchhausen*, directed by Josef von Báky. Goebbels wanted this film to celebrate the twenty-fifth anniversary of the UFA film studio. Practically every available candle in Berlin was requisitioned to shoot the scene at the court of Catherine the Great. Meissen porcelain, gold cutlery, and furniture were carried from the various museums to the studio. An immense cake made its appearance at the far end of the long table of the tsarina's guests. On cutting the first slice of the cake, the height of a guard captain, it could be seen to be hollow, and inside a dwarf was playing the harpsichord. The footmen behind the guests were played by members of the SS: it was thought they would be more discreet about divulging what was happening there. But there is no trace of the Reich in any scene: the film is an eccentric picture of old Europe, the story of a man who wants just to live, who has no wish for power since it would disturb him, and he lands on the moon like Judy Garland going to the wizard of Oz. At the beginning, ladies and gentlemen dance a minuet. For a few moments the film appears to be an accurate, rather tedious, historical film. The musicians then, without a break, move delicately on to play a tango. The couples take hold of each other, wigged heads move closer together. When the story moves back to the eighteenth-century adventures of Münchhausen, each take contains an enthralling abrasion: nonreality. We encounter Cagliostro, Casanova, Blanchard in much the same way as Münchhausen on the cannonball: they no longer touch the ground, but have the fragile luster of decalcomania. And we are captivated by such images as Isabella d'Este in the arms of the invisible baron, who crosses the hall of the astonished harem in midair.

When *Münchhausen* was premiered at a gala evening at the UFA Palast in Berlin, Goebbels had personally arranged the seating. The director, Veit Harlan, found himself seated in the first row of the stalls, while his wife, Kristina Söderbaum, was in the first row of the balcony. Goebbels gave a speech on the history and achievements of the UFA, just as he had spoken two weeks before at the Sportpalast to announce "total war."

"Later we met up at the villa of Professor Carl Froelich. There were Hans Albers, the director von Báky, Wolfgang Liebeneiner, and finally Goebbels also arrived. There was much talk about Erich Kästner [who had written the script for *Münchhausen* under a false name, as he was banned by the regime]. Goebbels was most intrigued by him. If I am not mistaken, Goebbels had originally had some difficulty with the Chancellery of the Reich in getting him accepted as the screenwriter. Kästner had after all written the poem on the First World War that said: 'If we had won the war . . . But fortunately we haven't.' Goebbels had read much of Kästner's writings and told us: 'It would be a great folly to get rid of people like Kästner. German art much needs intelligence like his, and intelligence is readily lacking among Germans. I had problems over Kästner—thank goodness I was able to overcome them.'"

March 9, 1943. Tunis racked by bombings. Outcome of the war still uncertain. Gide still sees Hitler and Stalin as the leaders of two countries that "have done much to free us" from something not too clear that is described as the "mythological era" (elsewhere he talks about a "mythological numbness"). A benevolent labor, which may appear "iniquitous and cruel" to those who nevertheless "will benefit tomorrow from the immense advantages" thus obtained. It is pointless insisting on certain brutal aspects of what is happening: they are "wounds of a day, over which the flesh heals and the honesty of tomorrow can be reestablished." Gide adds: "This is what Stalin and Hitler can say, and which they have some reason to think." But not just they. Gide thinks so too: "And this is also what I repeat to myself endlessly, what my head answers back to my heart."

April 1943. Curzio Malaparte had gone back as war correspondent to follow the siege of Leningrad. From the banks of the vast Lake Ladoga, "the presence of Leningrad is not so much felt as divined. [. . .] It is none the less a living presence: a mute presence lurking behind the high, compact wall of the forest." And the forest absorbs everything within, "savage and ruthless, it dominates, devours, crushes everything. Here the smell of man gives way to the much stronger smell, at once pungent and sweet, the thin, cold smell of the foliage." Until something human appeared: "The first human image that emerged from that cold, bare, elemental scene was extraordinary beyond belief. Like two demons lying in ambush, like two 'black angels' expelled from heaven by an irate Divinity, like two miserable, pitiful Lucifers, the bodies of two Soviet parachutists dangled side by side from the branches of two fir-trees. A party of Finnish soldiers was bringing up ladders and various implements with which to take down the bodies and bury them. [. . .] It resembled one of those scenes portrayed by the Italian primitives, in which the figurations of 'black angels' were calculated to inspire the beholder with a feeling of religious horror. And, indeed, it was a feeling of religious horror that I experienced now: as if there had appeared before my eyes concrete evidence of the wrath of God, the last scene of a drama enacted in some exalted, superhuman realm, the epilogue to a tragedy of pride, to a betrayal, to a revolt of 'black angels.'"

April 9, 1943. Goebbels notes in his diary: "Polish mass graves have been found near Smolensk. The Bolsheviks here have simply shot dead and buried in mass graves around 10,000 Polish prisoners, including civilian prisoners, bishops, intellectuals, artists, etc. Over these mass graves they have planted flowerbeds to blot out all trace of their iniquitous enterprise. Thanks to the indications of the local inhabitants the secret of these executions has been discovered, and a frightening devastation of human life is now revealed." This was Katyń. The number indicated by Goebbels was only a first estimate, a low approximation. The Red Army, following directives in the Beria memorandum of March 1940, had killed 21,857 Polish prisoners. Eight thousand of these were army officers. And since every Polish university graduate automatically became an army officer, killing them meant eliminating a large part of the country's current and future ruling class.

The name Katyń appears in Goebbels's diary on April 28. It became "the Katyń case," an argument to be used "with cunning and skill" to open rifts between the allies. At that point, indeed, the Polish government in exile in London broke off relations with the USSR. Stalin declared that he was outraged by the slanderous reconstruction of events at Katyń. The massacre must have been carried out by the Germans. But the disruptive effect of the rift, on which Goebbels was relying, is minimal. The Allies have not a moment's doubt when it comes to choosing between the USSR and the Polish government. They follow Stalin.

Meanwhile the German military authorities manage to prevent the appearance of newsreel pictures of Katyń. Too similar to our own—this is the underlying thinking. When Goebbels was able to see them, he found them "so horrifying that they are only partly fit to be made public." And yet Goebbels wanted them to be seen—and for Hitler to see them. But "unfortunately the Führer has not had the time to look at them personally and wants to broadcast them perhaps in the next newsreel. Yet by then the pictures will be so out of date that they will have no further news value." Goebbels is sorry about this. But the military authorities insist the pictures are not to be broadcast. Goebbels concludes: "The military authorities, in this regard, are concerned principally about the feelings of the families of our war dead. We must therefore choose between having regard for these compatriots or for the general interests of the German people. I place the latter higher and am therefore in favor of showing Bolshevism as it is."

April 11, 1943. The German Trans-Ocean news agency reports the discovery of the mass grave at Katyń with the bodies of around 3,000 Polish officers killed by the NKVD in March 1940. It is followed, two days later, by a radio communiqué from Berlin, which added certain details and was reported internationally. The Soviets replied on April 15 with a communiqué issued by the Sovinformburo describing the claims by "Goebbels's slanderers" as "monstrous" and accusing the Germans of having carried out the massacre themselves in the summer of 1941, after the withdrawal of Soviet troops from the area of Smolensk. That same day, General Sikorski, head of the Polish government in exile, demanded explanations from the Soviet embassy and urged the International Red Cross to open an investigation. Then, together with Foreign Minister Raczyński, he met Churchill for breakfast at Downing Street. Churchill told them he believed the Soviets were guilty, but advised against publicizing the matter. Sikorski replied that he couldn't avoid it.

On April 16, at 9 a.m., the secretary of the Polish Red Cross, Kazimierz Skarżyński, arrived at Katyń: "In the clearing between the graves lay the corpses of our officers that had been exhumed thus far, and large Red Cross flags were spread out above the graves. There was no doubt whatever that we were dealing with a mass execution carried out by an experienced executioner's hand. All the corpses that I saw had an entry wound from a revolver bullet at the base of the skull and an exit wound on the forehead or face. The uniform character of the wounds and the direction of the shots indicate that they were made from small arms at the smallest possible distance from the officers, who were standing up. Some of the corpses had their arms tied behind their backs with strong rope. They were probably men who defended themselves. Polish uniforms, badges, decorations, regimental insignia, overcoats, trousers, and boots were well preserved despite contact with the earth and decomposition. Lower down, deep in the excavated pits, there were more layers of corpses, and one could see skulls, legs, hands, and backs sticking out of the tightly pressed earth." The date of the killings could be deduced from the height of the young pines that had grown on the graves. On the victims, the Soviets had left identity documents and diaries, all of which ended in the early days of April 1940.

July 24, 1943. Paolo Monelli was curious about everything; with his inquisitive monocle he wanted to follow what was happening while it was happening. That afternoon he visited Roberto Suster, director of Agenzia Stefani, to get a feel of how the wind was blowing. Suster was anxious, he kept saying that Mussolini was "mad, mad in the head, he is no longer able to think, apathetic, irresponsible." Monelli then wanted to go "to have a look at Piazza Venezia. It was deserted, a few people were hanging about, cautiously, on street corners; odd civilians were grouped here and there, and it was immediately apparent who they were, they were the same people who, while Mussolini was watching maneuvers on the Apennines, were posing as if on vacation, strange vacationers who at high noon spent hours halfway up a mountain getting burnt by the sun; they were the same who at Stresa were pretending to be fishermen; but always dressed in the same way, with that international uniform of all policemen in the world, as my friend Xammar, special envoy for the *Ahora* of Madrid, wrote, 'boina, bastón, impermeable, y manos sucias.'"

But the day hadn't yet finished. And days always finished at the café, the one where the intellectuals went: "At Caffè Aragno, between nine and ten o'clock, regular customers, journalists, artists and writers are in lively discussion; it is curious to see that many still have their usual Fascist badges in the buttonholes of their white or gray jackets. The poet Cardarelli is hidden away in a corner, static, extraneous to the tumult, 'solitary above the fates,' he would say of himself, as befits God and a poet. A journalist asks 'What do you think?,' addressing him with the formal *Lei*. A senior military man nearby, in uniform, armed, turns around abruptly, 'People don't use *Lei* anymore,' he shouts. 'I speak as I please,' replies the journalist, the other retorts:

'What's got into you tonight, you all seem crazy?' two or
three back him up, Mario Pannunzio smashes a chair over
his head, the scuffle spreads, trays fly, tables overturned,
bottles broken, the army officer is no longer to be seen, buried under a pyramid of chairs; at this moment Corrado
Sofia, a Sicilian, comes in breathless, 'they've arrested Mussolini,' he shouts, 'they've arrested Mussolini,' it seems like
the finale of *Cavalleria Rusticana*. The commotion turns into
a bedlam of hurrahs, shouting, hugging, everyone pouring
out onto the street, they want to rush to the newspaper offices for more news."

September 9, 1943. Norman Lewis, officer in the
312th Field Security Section, landed in Paestum at seven
in the evening. "An extraordinary false serenity lay on the
landward view," are Lewis's first words in Italy. Looking
around, "here and there, motionless columns of smoke de-
noted the presence of war, but the general impression was
one of a splendid and tranquil evening in the late summer
on one of the fabled shores of antiquity." And there was
someone in wait: "The corpses of those killed earlier in
the day had been laid out in a row, side by side, shoulder to
shoulder, with extreme precision as if about to present
arms at an inspection by death."

October 6, 1943. The *Gauleiter* meeting in Poznań is a
solemn event. General Milch speaks on behalf of the Luft-
waffe, Admiral Dönitz for the navy, Minister Speer for
armaments. Himmler speaks last, between five and six
thirty in the afternoon. A pragmatic speech that deals first

with specific problems and gradually widens up to prospects for the future. First, questions to be settled: partisans,
sabotage attacks, General Vlasov, who had defected to the
German side: "After three days we told the general more or
less this: You know very well you can't go back. But you're
an important man and we guarantee that, when the war is
over, you will have the pension of a Russian general, and
from now on you can have alcohol, cigarettes and women.
A man like this can be bought with very little. It costs very
little. You see, in these cases you have to be tremendously
cold in your calculations. A man like this costs 20,000
marks a year. If you keep him for ten or fifteen years, that
makes 300,000 marks. But even a military battery that
shoots properly for two days will cost 300,000 marks."

Other problems: paratroopers, the Slavs, the Russians,
work camps for prisoners of war. Step by step, Himmler
was approaching what he described as "the most difficult
problem of my life": the Jews. Everyone around him was
well aware that they would not have endured the "fourth
and perhaps the fifth and sixth year of war" if they still had
"this demoralizing pest in our national body." But it wasn't
just a matter of no longer seeing Jews in their own Gau, in
their own district. "Gentlemen, the phrase: 'The Jews
must be exterminated,' with its brevity, is easy to say. But,
for the man who has to carry out what it requires, it is the
hardest and most serious phrase there is." From this point
onward—apart from a few sarcastic words about the many
people who came to plead in favor of certain "famous decent Jews" ("the number [of decent Jews] seems even

higher than that of the whole Jewish population")—
Himmler's speech assumes another tone, the tone of secrecy:
"I beg you to listen to what I am telling you in this gathering and never to repeat it." Immediately then, a question:
"What about the women and children?" And the answer: "I
did not feel authorized to exterminate the men—that is to
say, to kill them or to have them killed—and to let the
children grow up to avenge themselves on our children and
grandchildren." And so, once again, Himmler had chosen
"a very clear solution." But there was a danger that "our
men and our leaders would suffer mental and spiritual harm.
A very close danger." They had to avoid, at the same time,
becoming "brutal, heartless" or "soft" and liable to nervous
breakdown. "This path between Scylla and Charybdis is
tremendously narrow." He wanted to state, however, that
"the Jewish problem in the lands we have occupied will be
solved by the end of the year. Only residual matters will
remain, of individual Jews who are living in hiding."

But that was not all. Himmler wanted to end on the
Jewish question, but he knew that something could *still* not
be said: "Now you are aware of the situation and will keep
everything to yourselves. Perhaps one day, much later on,
one might consider the possibility of saying something more
to the German people. But the best thing, I believe, is that
we—all of us—have supported this weight for our people,
that we have shouldered the responsibility ourselves (the responsibility for an action and not just for an idea) and that
then we carry the secret to our graves."

October 16, 1943. A busy day for Ernst Jünger. He is thinking about the machine as a "predator whose danger was not immediately recognized by man." He regards technology as a "construction built on land not sufficiently explored." He browses through an eighteenth-century account of famous trials and stops at a phrase regarding Madame de Brinvilliers, the incomparable poisoner: "Great crimes, far from being suspected, are not even imagined." They seem digressions—and are a prelude.

A visit from Bogo, the name behind which Jünger hides Friedrich Hielscher, an old companion of conspiracies. The pseudonym alludes to the gnostic Bogomil sect. And indeed Bogo, notes Jünger, "has founded a church." He is elaborating its doctrine, while the liturgy is already established. It includes "a cycle of festivals, 'the Pagan Year,' which envisages a system of relationships between gods, festivals, colors, animals, food, stones and plants." It is the archaic system of correspondences that arises through the will of an individual who decides every detail.

Bogo had no confidence in the military conspiracies against Hitler. He thought he should act for himself, "like an Old Man of the Mountain, who sends his young men to the palaces." But Bogo didn't just talk about that. Meanwhile he was unpacking a series of carved pipes, with a "mischievous and inquisitive" air. Jünger, who knew him well, understood that in his behavior there was a hidden motive: "I had the impression that he chose the pipes as the progression of the speech required." There was a progression—and it was moving toward a climax. During his travels—Bogo continued—he had been to Łódź. A hundred and twenty thousand Jews lived in the ghetto and were making weapons. It was the only way of delaying, by little, their elimination. "To make them vanish, cremation ovens have been built close to the ghetto."

But, Bogo continued, "it seems there is a second form of extermination, which consists of this: before burning them, they make their victims climb, naked, onto a large iron plate, where the electrical current is passed. This method has been arrived at because it was discovered that the SS charged with firing the shot to the back of the head were suffering nervous disorders and in the end refused. These cremation ovens require a limited staff; it is said they are worked by some kind of diabolical leaders and their servants. That is where the masses of Jews deported from Europe to 'settle elsewhere' disappear." Only on that day would Jünger find out, through Bogo, about the existence of extermination camps.

October 24, 1943. A new urgent task for Missie Vassiltchikov in her office: "The translation of the captions for a large number of photographs of the remains of some 4,000 Polish officers found murdered by the Soviets in Katyń forest near Smolensk. The mind boggles." And all is surrounded by secrecy. Missie manages to work out that von Papen, ambassador to Ankara, has "authorized a member of his staff to become chummy with a Polish diplomatic representative in Turkey who, in his turn, is a friend of Steve Early's, President Roosevelt's special representative there." It seems that "Roosevelt has expressed the wish to receive the full, unadulterated story—a thing he is, apparently, unable to do in the States because his entourage (Morgenthau?) intercept and suppress any report unfavorable to the Soviet Union. The translations must be ready in two days. I feel very strange when I think that my prose will land on President Roosevelt's desk in less than a week."

November 1943. Clothes are rationed in Berlin, but not women's hats. Missie Vassiltchikov makes the most of it. "We are slowly accumulating them." Even later, Missie would manage to pick up a Rose Valois hat, "a large, bright green sombrero with black ribbons," that someone had sent to her sister Tatiana. And she wouldn't forget about hats even when the Battle of Berlin was raging: "The morning after the first raid I had had an appointment to try on a hat at a small neighborhood shop. All around the houses were burning, but I wanted that hat badly and so I now went over and rang the bell and, wonder of wonders, was met by a smiling saleswoman: 'Durchlaucht können anprobieren!' ['Your Highness may try it on!']. I did so, but as I was wearing muddy slacks it was difficult to judge the effect."

May 18, 1944. Noel Willmett was not convinced that "totalitarianism, leader-worship, etc.," were really on the increase, seeing that they didn't seem to be establishing themselves in Britain and the United States. Orwell replied, looking ahead to the years after the war, "Already history has in a sense ceased to exist, ie. there is no such thing as a history of our own times which could be universally accepted. [. . .] Hitler can say that the Jews started the war, and if he survives that will become official history. He can't say that two and two are five, because for the purpose of, say, ballistics they have to make four. But if the sort of world that I am afraid of arrives, a world of two or three great superstates which are unable to conquer one another, two and two could become five if the fuhrer wished it. That, so far as I can see, is the direction in which we are actually moving, though, of course, the process is reversible."

September 1944. Vasily Grossman arrives in Treblinka with General Chuikov's troops from Stalingrad, thirteen months after the extermination camp revolt. On Himmler's orders all the buildings had been demolished in a vain attempt to make the place unrecognizable. But traces of the dead were apparent everywhere. The ashes were carted away by peasants, along a road that had become black "like a mourning ribbon. [. . .] Each day twenty carts made six to eight trips; during each trip they scattered 120 to 130 kilos of ash." And then there was the soil. "Lupins were sown on the site of the camp, and a settler by the name of Streben built himself a little house there. Now this house has gone; it too was burned down." The earth "is casting up fragments of bone, teeth, sheets of paper, clothes, things of all kinds. The earth does not want to keep secrets." Grossman moved on, over the field of lupins: "We walk on over the swaying, bottomless earth of Treblinka and suddenly come to a stop. Thick wavy hair, gleaming like burnished copper, the delicate lovely hair of a young woman, trampled into the ground; and beside it, some equally fine blond hair; and then some heavy black plaits on the bright sand; and then, more and more . . . Evidently these are the contents of a sack, just a single sack that somehow got left behind. Yes, it is all true. The last hope, the last wild hope that it was all just a terrible dream, has gone. And the lupin pods keep popping open, and the tiny peas keep pattering down—and this really does all sound like a funeral knell rung by countless little bells from under the earth."

September 5, 1944. In his wanderings through Germany, together with his wife, Lucette, their cat Bébert, and his friend Le Vigan, Céline reaches Berlin from Baden-Baden and writes to Paul Bonny: "After our departure from Baden-Baden we have lived in a nightmare, not bombings, but what sights! What nightmare! Berlin bewitched to suicide. The place is irresistible. All in all, any cemetery is a laugh, a joke in comparison to this incredible horror."

April 1945. Soldiers of the Red Army—who were coming from years of great hardship and from a country where very little worked, and the little that did work was dreadful—looked about as they advanced through Germany. According to Grossman: "It was in Germany, particularly here in Berlin, that our soldiers really started to ask themselves why did the Germans attack us so suddenly? Why did the Germans need this terrible and unfair war? Millions of our men have now seen the rich farms in East Prussia, the highly organized agriculture, the concrete sheds for livestock, spacious rooms, carpets, wardrobes full of clothes. Millions of our soldiers have seen the well-built roads running from one village to another and German autobahns . . . Our soldiers have seen the two-storey suburban houses with electricity, gas, bathrooms and beautifully tended gardens. Our people have seen the villas of the rich bourgeoisie in Berlin, the unbelievable luxury of castles, estates and mansions. And thousands of soldiers repeat these angry questions when they look around them in Germany: 'But why did they come to us? What did they want?'"

April 1945. Grossman arrives at Berlin with Colonel General Berzarin, the first to enter the city: "Fat, brown-eyed, arch, with white hair although he is young. He is clever, very calm and resourceful." Marshal Zhukov appoints him commander of Berlin.

Shortly before the city's surrender, Grossman finds himself in the castle of the von Treskow family at Friedrichsfelde: "Evening. Park. Half-dark rooms. A clock is chiming. China. Colonel Petrov has a bad toothache. Fireplace. Through the windows can be heard artillery fire and the howling of Katyushas. Suddenly, there is thunder from the skies. The sky is yellow and cloudy. It is warm, rainy, there is an odor of lilac. There's an old pond in the park. The silhouettes of the statues are indistinct. I am sitting in an armchair by the fireplace. The clock is chiming, infinitely sad and melodic, like poetry itself. I am holding an old book in my hands. Fine pages. Written in a trembling, apparently old man's, hand is 'von Treskow.' He must have been the owner." According to the family, the book belonged to Münthe von Treskow. Soviet troops had thrown him out of the castle. He then died of starvation.

May 2, 1945. Berlin has fallen. "Fires and fires, smoke, smoke, smoke. [. . .] Among the ruins, in flames, amid hundreds of corpses in the streets. Corpses squashed by tanks, squeezed out like tubes. Almost all of them are clutching grenades and sub-machine guns in their hands. They have been killed fighting. Most of the dead men are dressed in brown shirts. They were Party activists who defended the approaches to the Reichstag and the Reichschancellery." Into which Grossman sets foot, together with Efim Gekhman, his comrade from Stalingrad, "to whom God, evidently, forgot to transmit the sense of fear." In Hitler's study, Grossman opens the drawer of a desk and takes out some rubber stamps bearing the words "'The Führer has confirmed,' 'The Führer has agreed.'" Today those stamps form part of the writer's estate.

III

SIGHTING OF
THE TOWERS

On a lone, undated sheet of paper, now in the Biblio-thèque Jacques Doucet, Baudelaire describes the collapse of an immense tower that one day would be called a sky-scraper. He felt a sense of powerlessness because he could not transmit the news to the "people," to the "nations." So he had to be content with murmuring it to the "more intelligent." But even this murmur had to wait more than a century to be printed. And no one noticed it. The "nations" didn't realize in time what was awaiting them. It had all happened in a dream, in one of those dreams that Baudelaire was accustomed to: those dreams that make you never want to sleep again:

"Symptoms of ruin. Immense buildings. Many, one on the other, apartments, rooms, *temples*, galleries, stairs, bow-els, belvederes, lanterns, fountains, statues.—*Fissures, cracks. Humidity that comes from a cistern situated close to the sky.*—How to warn the people, the nations—? we warn in an ear of the more intelligent.

"At the top, a column gives way and the two extremi-ties move. Nothing has yet collapsed. I can no longer find the way out. I go down, then back up again. *A tower-labyrinth.*

I never managed to get out. I live forever in a building that's about to collapse, a building infected by a secret disease.—I calculate, inside me, to amuse myself, whether such a prodigious mass of stones, marble, statues, walls that are about to smash against each other will be very much smeared by the great quantity of brain matter, of human flesh and of shattered bones." When the "news" of this dream reached the "nations," it all corresponded, but with one single addition: the towers were two—and were twins.

NOTES

The first number refers to the page, the second to the line of text where the quotation ends.

3, 5   Roberto Calasso, *The Ruin of Kasch*, Farrar, Straus and Giroux, New York, 2018, p. 267.

7, 7   "The Kafir's Blood Is Halal for You, So Shed It," in *Rumiyah*, September 2016, p. 34.

7, 13 Ibid., p. 36.

7, 27 M. G. S. Hodgson, *The Order of Assassins*, Mouton & Co., 's-Gravenhage, 1955, p. 50.

8, 14 Marco Polo, *Milione*, edited by V. Bertolucci Pizzorusso, Adelphi, Milan, 1975, p. 56.

8, 17 Loc. cit.

8, 19 Ibid., p. 57.

8, 28 Ibid., p. 58.

9, 20 Friedrich Nietzsche, *Zur Genealogie der Moral*, in *Sämtliche Werke. Kritische Studienausgabe*, edited by G. Colli and M. Montinari, dtv-de Gruyter, Berlin-Munich, second revised edition, 1988, vol. V, p. 399 (III, 24).

10, 4 Joseph von Hammer-Purgstall, *Die Geschichte der Assassinen*, J. G. Cotta'schen Buchhandlung, Stuttgart-Tübingen, 1818, p. 84.

10, 13 Nicolas de Staël, in Betty Bouthoul, *Le Vieux de la Montagne*, Gallimard, Paris, 1958, p. 7.

11, 11 F. Battistini, "Le donne della virtù che frustano i 'vizi,'" in *Sette*, October 7, 2016, p. 51.

12, 19 Lawrence Wright, *The Looming Tower*, Knopf, New York, 2006, p. 22.

13, 21 A. B. al-Mehri, Introduction to Sayyid Qutb, *Milestones* (1964), edited by A. B. al-Mehri, Maktabah, Birmingham, 2006, p. 13.

14, 11 Sayyid Qutb, *Milestones*, American Trust Publications, Indianapolis, 1990, p. 5.

17, 28 Jacob Burckhardt, *Griechische Kulturgeschichte, I*, in *Gesammelte Werke*, Schwabe, Basel-Stuttgart, vol. V, 1978, p. 93.

18, 9 Jacob Burckhardt, *Kulturgeschichte Griechenlands*, Deutsche Buch-Gemeinschaft, Berlin, 1940, p. vii.

18, 17 Jacob Burckhardt, *Griechische Kulturgeschichte, I*, cit., p. 92.

18, 19 Ibid., p. 93.

21, 14 Émile Durkheim, *The Elementary Forms of Religious Life*, Free Press, New York, 1995 (trans. Karen E. Fields), p. 356.

22, 4 Ibid., p. 445.

22, 9 Émile Durkheim, "Saint-Simon, fondateur du positivisme et de la sociologie," in *Revue Philosophique de la France et de l'Étranger*, XCIX, January-June 1925, p. 321.

22, 23 Émile Durkheim, *The Elementary Forms of Religious Life*, cit., p. 208.

23, 12 Plato, *Republic*, 493 c.

23, 15 Simone Weil, *Cahiers* (December 1941–end January 1942), in *Œuvres complètes*, edited by A. A. Devaux and F. de Lussy, Gallimard, Paris, vol. VI, book ii, 1997, p. 378.

23, 19 Ibid., p. 132.

23, 22 Simone Weil, *Cahiers* (April 26—June 7, 1942), in *Œuvres complètes*, cit., vol. VI, book iii, 2002, p. 395.

24, 29 Ludwig Wittgenstein, "Remarks on Frazer's *Golden Bough*" (1931), in *Philosophical Occasions, 1912–1951*, edited

NOTES

by J. C. Klagge and A. Nordmann, Hackett, Indianapolis, 1993, p. 129.

25, 13 Osip Mandelstam, "Gumanizm i sovremennost'," in *Nakanune: Literaturnoe priloženie* 36, January 20, 1923, p. 6; "Humanism and the Present," in *The Complete Critical Prose and Letters*, edited by J. G. Harris, Ardis, Ann Arbor, 1979, p. 181.

25, 22 Loc. cit.

25, 27 Henry Kissinger, *World Order*, Penguin Books, New York, 2014, p. 2.

26, 12 Ibid., p. 8.

27, 14 Akbar Ganji, "Who Is Ali Khamenei?" in *Foreign Affairs* XCII, September–October 2013, p. 29.

27, 23 Henry Kissinger, *World Order*, cit., p. 346.

27, 28 Loc. cit.

28, 16 George Orwell, *1984*, Harcourt Brace Jovanovich, San Diego, New York, and London, 1949, p. 35.

33, 21 "Catéchisme du révolutionnaire" (1869), in M. Confino, *Violence dans la violence*, François Maspero, Paris, 1973, p. 104.

35, 4 Alexis de Tocqueville, *De la démocratie en Amérique*, Charles Gosselin, Paris, vol. IV, 1840, p. 290.

35, 9 Loc. cit.

35, 19 Nicolas Malebranche, *Traité de la nature et de la grâce* (1680), in *Œuvres*, edited by G. Rodis-Lewis, Gallimard, Paris, vol. II, 1992, p. 109.

36, 8 Peter of Celle, *De conscientia*, 91–92, in *Selected Works*, Cistercian Publications, Kalamazoo (Michigan), 1987, pp. 184–85.

40, 15 Friedrich Nietzsche, *Der Gottesdienst der Griechen* (1875–1878), in *Werke. Kritische Gesamtausgabe*, edited by F. Bornmann and M. Carpitella, de Gruyter, Berlin, section II, vol. V, 1995, p. 364.

42, 24 John Stuart Mill, *Autobiography*, Longmans, Green, Reader, and Dyer, London, 1873, p. 43.

43, 9   Ibid., pp. 40–41.

43, 17   Gottfried Wilhelm Leibniz, *Essais de Théodicée* (1710), in *Die philosophischen Schriften*, edited by C. J. Gerhardt, Olms, Hildesheim, vol. VI, 1965, p. 114.

45, 13   Hugo von Hofmannsthal, *Andreas*, in *Gesammelte Werke*, edited by B. Schoeller and R. Hirsch, S. Fischer, Frankfurt a. M., vol. VII, 1979, p. 271.

48, 4   Charles Baudelaire, "Sur la Belgique," in *Œuvres complètes*, edited by C. Pichois, Gallimard, Paris, vol. II, 1976, p. 899.

48, 21   Simone Weil, "L'Iliade' ou le poème de la force," in *Œuvres complètes*, cit., vol. II, book iii, 1989, p. 251.

49, 4   Simone Weil, "Intuitions pré-chrétiennes," in *Œuvres complètes*, cit., vol. IV, book ii, 2009, p. 291.

49, 6   Loc. cit.

49, 8   Ibid., p. 292.

50, 10   Virgil, *Aeneid*, I, 405.

51, 1   John Stuart Mill, *Autobiography*, cit., pp. 132–33.

51, 5   Ibid., p. 133.

51, 6   Loc. cit.

51, 11   Ibid., pp. 133–34.

51, 12   Ibid., p. 134.

51, 14   Loc. cit.

51, 15   Ibid., p. 133.

51, 23   Ibid., pp. 139–40.

51, 30   Samuel Taylor Coleridge, "Dejection: An Ode," line 21, in *The Poems of Samuel Taylor Coleridge*, edited by E. H. Coleridge, Oxford University Press, London, 1912, p. 364.

60, 6   Genesis, 7:8.

60, 9   Koran, 17:87.

63, 21   Constantine Cavafy, "Half an Hour," line 7, Princeton University Press, 1972 (trans. Edmund Keeley and Philip Sherrard), p. 37.

NOTES

63, 26 Gottfried Benn, *Der Ptolemäer* (1949), in *Sämtliche Werke*, edited by G. Schuster and I. Benn, Klett-Cotta, Stuttgart, vol. V, 1991, p. 24.

65, 6 D. J. Chalmers, synopsis of *Its from Bits*, January 27, 2017, p. 2.

65, 15 D. J. Chalmers, "The Mind Bleeds into the World," in *Edge*, January 24, 2017.

67, 1 Letter from Gottfried Wilhelm Leibniz to Antoine Verjus, August 18, 1705, in J. Baruzi, *Leibniz*, Bloud, Paris, 1909, p. 155.

67, 8 Loc. cit.

67, 26 Loc. cit.

69, 29 René Guénon, *Orient et Occident* (1924), Éditions de la Maisnie, Paris, 1987, pp. 67–68.

75, 24 Yuval Noah Harari, *Homo Deus*, Harvill Secker, London, 2016, p. 380.

76, 18 Mark O'Connell, *To Be a Machine*, Granta, London, 2017, p. 49.

77, 8 Yuval Noah Harari, *Homo Deus*, cit., p. 386.

77, 18 Ibid., p. 395.

77, 20 Ibid., p. 393.

77, 25 Ibid., p. 394.

78, 3 Ibid., p. 396.

78, 4 Loc. cit.

78, 14 Gregory Chaitin, *Meta Math!*, Pantheon Books, New York, 2005, pp. 60–61.

78, 17 Ibid., pp. 61–62.

78, 26 Michael A. Nielsen, "The Bits That Make Up the Universe," in *Nature* CDXXVII, 2004, p. 16.

79, 5 D. J. Chalmers, synopsis of *Its from Bits*, cit., p. 1.

79, 17 Gregory Chaitin, *Meta Math!*, cit., p. 114.

79, 24 Ibid., p. 87.

79, 28 Loc. cit.

81, 2 Simone Weil, *À propos de la mécanique ondulatoire*, in *Œuvres complètes*, cit., vol. IV, book i, 2008, p. 493.

81, 5 Ibid., p. 494.

81, 10 Loc. cit.

82, 25 Stuart Russell, synopsis of *Beneficial Intelligence*, May 9, 2017, p. 1.

82, 26 Loc. cit.

82, 28 Ibid., p. 2.

83, 1 Loc. cit.

83, 13 Adam Smith, *An Inquiry into the Nature and Causes of the Wealth of Nations*, W. Strahan and T. Cadell, London, vol. I, 1776, p. 415.

83, 23 Stuart Russell, synopsis of *Beneficial Intelligence*, cit., p. 1.

84, 2 Loc. cit.

86, 2 Walter Benjamin, "Franz Kafka," in *Illuminations*, edited by Hannah Arendt (trans. Harry Zorn), Pimlico, London, 1999, p. 130.

86, 5 Letter from Theodor W. Adorno to Walter Benjamin, December 16, 1934, in Walter Benjamin, *Gesammelte Schriften*, cit., vol. II, book iii, 1977, p. 1173.

86, 7 Walter Benjamin, "Der Sürrealismus" (1929), in *Gesammelte Schriften*, cit., vol. II, book i, 1977, p. 307.

86, 17 Loc. cit.

86, 27 Loc. cit.

88, 17 Robert Frost, Introduction to E.A. Robinson's *King Jasper* (1935), in *Collected Poems, Prose, and Plays*, edited by R. Poirier and M. Richardson, Library of America, New York, 1995, p. 743.

93, 10 Klaus Mann, *Der Wendepunkt* (1942), S. Fischer, Frankfurt a. M., 1952, p. 298.

93, 12 Loc. cit.

93, 16 Loc. cit.

93, 19 Robert Brasillach, *Notre Avant-guerre*, Plon, Paris, 1941, p. 131.

93, 20 Loc. cit.

94, 6 Loc. cit.

94, 22 Ibid., p. 129.

94, 27 Georges Simenon, "Europe 33" (1933), in *Mes apprentissages*, edited by F. Lacassin, Omnibus, Paris, 2016, p. 762.

95, 14 Ibid., p. 763.

95, 20 Letter from Walter Benjamin to Gershom Scholem, March 20, 1933, in *Gesammelte Briefe*, edited by Ch. Gödde and H. Lonitz, Suhrkamp, Frankfurt a. M., vol. IV, 1998, p. 169.

95, 23 Ibid., p. 170.

95, 25 Virginia Woolf, note of April 29, 1933, in *The Diary of Virginia Woolf*, edited by A. O. Bell with the collaboration of A. McNeillie, Penguin, London, vol. IV, 1983, p. 153.

96, 13 Loc. cit.

96, 15 Loc. cit.

96, 26 Letter from Louis-Ferdinand Céline to Cillie Ambor, spring 1933, in *Lettres*, edited by H. Godard and J.-P. Louis, Gallimard, Paris, 2009, p. 364.

96, 29 Letter from Louis-Ferdinand Céline to Cillie Ambor, April 20, 1933, ibid., p. 366.

97, 10 M. Martin du Gard, *Les Mémorables (1918–1945)*, Gallimard, Paris, 1999, p. 840.

97, 14 Letter from Louis-Ferdinand Céline to Eugène Dabit of May 1933, in *Lettres*, cit., p. 369.

97, 24 Letter from Louis-Ferdinand Céline to Élie Faure, May 1933, ibid., p. 375.

98, 2 Letter from Joseph Roth to Stefan Zweig, May 9, 1933, in J. Roth–S. Zweig, *"Jede Freundschaft mit mir ist verderblich." Briefwechsel 1927–1938*, edited by M. Rietra and R. J. Siegel, Wallstein, Göttingen, 2011, p. 103.

98, 24 Letter from Joseph Roth to Stefan Zweig, May 22, 1933, ibid., pp. 105–106.

98, 28 M. Martin du Gard, *Les Mémorables*, cit., p. 848.

99, 5   Loc. cit.

99, 6   Ibid., p. 849.

99, 12 Loc. cit.

100, 3 Jörg Lanz von Liebenfels, *Der elektrische Urgott und sein großes Heiligtum in der Vorzeit*, Hertersburg-Versand, Prerow-Pommern, 1933, cover.

100, 12 Pierre Drieu La Rochelle, *Socialisme fasciste*, Gallimard, Paris, 1934, p. 162.

100, 23 Ibid., p. 163.

101, 2 Letter from Louis-Ferdinand Céline to Élie Faure, March 18, 1934, in *Lettres*, cit., p. 416.

101, 4 Letter from Louis-Ferdinand Céline to Élie Faure, April 14, 1934, ibid., p. 417.

101, 11 Letter from Louis-Ferdinand Céline to Élie Faure, March 18, 1934, ibid., p. 416.

101, 19 Letter from Louis-Ferdinand Céline to Élie Faure, April 14, 1934, ibid., p. 418.

101, 25 Postcard from Louis-Ferdinand Céline to Elizabeth Craig, May 31, 1934, ibid., p. 425.

101, 27 Alphonse Juilland, *Elizabeth et Louis*, Gallimard, Paris, 1994, p. 341.

102, 14 Louis-Ferdinand Céline, *Voyage au bout de la nuit*, Denoël et Steele, Paris, 1932, p. 7.

102, 24 Louis Untermeyer, in *The Letters of Robert Frost to Louis Untermeyer*, edited by L. Untermeyer, Holt, Rinehart and Winston, New York, Chicago, and San Francisco, 1963, p. 256.

102, 27 Letter from Robert Frost to Louis Untermeyer, February 17, 1935, ibid., p. 254.

102, 28 Loc. cit.

103, 2 Ibid., p. 255.

103, 4 Loc. cit.

103, 8 Loc. cit.

103, 15 Ibid., p. 256.

105, 4 Virginia Woolf, note of April 22, 1935, in *The Diary of Virginia Woolf*, cit., p. 304.

105, 21 Virginia Woolf, note of May 9, 1935, ibid., p. 311.

106, 4 Letter from Ernst Jünger to Carl Schmitt, June 4, 1935, in E. Jünger–C. Schmitt, *Briefe 1930–1983*, edited by H. Kiesel, Klett-Cotta, Stuttgart, 1999, p. 49.

106, 5 Letter from Carl Schmitt to Ernst Jünger, May 3, 1936, ibid., p. 57.

106, 12 Letter from Louis-Ferdinand Céline to Lucienne Delforge, August 26, 1935, in *Lettres*, cit., p. 466.

106, 25 Letter from Louis-Ferdinand Céline to Élie Faure, July 22 or 23, 1935, ibid., p. 462.

106, 28 Ibid., p. 463.

107, 11 Letter from Samuel Beckett to Mary Manning Howe, December 13, 1936, in *The Letters of Samuel Beckett*, edited by M. Dow Fehsenfeld and L. More Overbeck, Cambridge University Press, Cambridge, vol. I, 2009, p. 397.

107, 13 Samuel Beckett, "L'Expulsé" (1945), in *Nouvelles et textes pour rien*, Les Éditions de Minuit, Paris, 1955, p. 19.

107, 16 Loc. cit.

107, 22 Letter from Samuel Beckett to Günter Albrecht, December 31, 1936, in *The Letters of Samuel Beckett*, cit., p. 408.

107, 27 Letter from Samuel Beckett to Mary Manning Howe, March 21, 1937, ibid., p. 468.

108, 5 Letter from Samuel Beckett to Günter Albrecht, March 30, 1937, ibid., p. 480.

108, 7 Ibid., p. 478.

108, 8 Letter from Samuel Beckett to Thomas McGreevy, March 25, 1937, ibid., p. 470.

108, 10 Letter from Samuel Beckett to Günter Albrecht, March 30, 1937, ibid., p. 480.

108, 25 Letter from Samuel Beckett to Thomas McGreevy, November 28, 1936, ibid., p. 389.

108, 28 Loc. cit.

109, 5   Letter from Samuel Beckett to Thomas McGreevy, March 7, 1937, ibid., pp. 460–61.

109, 15 Letter from Roberto Bazlen to Ludovico Sain, September 10, 1936, private collection.

109, 21 Loc. cit.

110, 6   Max Picard, *Die Flucht vor Gott*, Eugen Rentsch, Erlenbach-Zürich, Leipzig, 1934, p. 43.

110, 12 Magrini (pseudonym of Aldo Garosci), "Inventario," in *Giustizia e libertà* V, 9 (March 4, 1938), p. 3.

110, 28 Élie Halévy, "L'Ère des tyrannies" (1936), in *L'Ère des tyrannies*, Gallimard, Paris, 1938, p. 214.

112, 21 Letter from Marcel Mauss to Élie Halévy, undated, ibid., pp. 230–31.

113, 1   Élie Halévy, *L'Ère des tyrannies*, cit., p. 221.

113, 16 Ibid., pp. 214–15.

114, 1   Ibid., p. 214.

114, 27 Ibid., p. 226.

115, 3   Ibid., p. 214.

115, 6   Loc. cit.

115, 8   Loc. cit.

115, 13 Loc. cit.

115, 22 Ibid., p. 225.

116, 3   Ibid., p. 226.

116, 7   M. Martin du Gard, *Les Mémorables*, cit., p. 113.

116, 16 Ibid., p. 959.

116, 25 Robert Brasillach, *Notre Avant-guerre*, cit., p. 264.

117, 2   Ibid., p. 265.

117, 3   Loc. cit.

117, 6   Loc. cit.

117, 11 Loc. cit.

117, 12 Ibid., p. 266.

117, 16 Loc. cit.

117, 17 Loc. cit.

117, 22 Loc. cit.

117, 26 Ibid., p. 267.

117, 28 Ibid., p. 268.

118, 1 Loc. cit.

118, 7 Loc. cit.

118, 11 Loc. cit.

118, 15 Loc. cit.

118, 18 Loc. cit.

118, 21 Ibid., p. 269.

118, 22 Loc. cit.

118, 24 Loc. cit.

118, 24 Loc. cit.

118, 26 Loc. cit.

119, 2 Ibid., pp. 272–73.

119, 7 Ibid., p. 273.

119, 9 Loc. cit.

119, 10 Loc. cit.

119, 14 Ibid., p. 274.

119, 23 Ibid., p. 275.

119, 27 Loc. cit.

119, 29 Loc. cit.

120, 3 Loc. cit.

120, 6 Ibid., p. 276.

120, 16 Loc. cit.

120, 22 Ibid., pp. 276–77.

120, 30 Ibid., p. 276.

121, 11 Ibid., p. 277.

121, 15 Ibid., p. 278.

122, 8 Hermann Rauschning, *The Voice of Destruction*, G. P. Putnam's Sons, New York, p. 275.

122, 21 Ibid., p. 248.

122, 24 Ibid., p. 252.

122, 29 Ibid., p. 237.

123, 20 Ernst Jünger, note of April 18, 1939, in *Sämtliche Werke*, Klett-Cotta, Stuttgart, vol. II: *Tagebücher (Strahlungen I)*, 1998, pp. 37–38.

123, 25 Ibid., p. 38.

123, 26 Loc. cit.

123, 27 Loc. cit.

124, 1 Loc. cit.

124, 4 Loc. cit.

124, 11 Loc. cit.

124, 19 Letter from Walter Benjamin to Margarete Steffin, June 1939, in *Gesammelte Briefe*, cit., vol. VI, 2000, pp. 294–95.

124, 24 Arthur Koestler, *Scum of the Earth* (1941), Eland, London, 1991, p. 30.

124, 28 Ibid., p. 31.

125, 10 Ibid., p. 34.

125, 23 Ibid., p. 13.

125, 28 Ibid., p. 39.

126, 3 Ibid., p. 40.

126, 16 Loc. cit.

127, 10 Giaime Pintor, *Doppio diario (1936–1943)*, edited by M. Serri, Einaudi, Torino, 1978, p. 72.

127, 14 Klaus Mann, *Der Wendepunkt*, cit., p. 423.

127, 21 Loc. cit.

127, 28 Ibid., p. 424.

128, 2 Arthur Koestler, *Scum of the Earth*, cit., p. 242.

128, 7 Loc. cit.

128, 12 Ibid., p. 170.

128, 21 Ibid., p. 242.

128, 22 Ibid., p. 244.

129, 14 Loc. cit.

129, 18 Simone Weil, "À propos de la mécanique ondulatoire," cit., p. 490.

129, 19 Ibid., p. 493.

129, 25 Ibid., p. 496.

130, 1   Ibid., p. 491.

130, 9   Simone Weil, "L'Enracinement," in *Œuvres complètes*, cit., vol. V, book ii, 2013, p. 312.

130, 11 Loc. cit.

130, 13 Loc. cit.

130, 21 Ibid., pp. 312–13.

131, 2   André Gide, note of January 12, 1941, in *Journal*, edited by M. Sagaert, Gallimard, Paris, vol. II: *1926–1950*, 1997, p. 748.

131, 5   Loc. cit.

131, 12 Loc. cit.

131, 14 Loc. cit.

131, 17 Loc. cit.

131, 22 Loc. cit.

131, 27 Marie Vassiltchikov, note of February 17, 1941, in *Berlin Diaries (1940–1945)*, Knopf, New York, 1987, p. 41.

132, 2   Marie Vassiltchikov, note of February 18, 1941, ibid., p. 41.

132, 9   Loc. cit.

132, 11 Marie Vassiltchikov, note of March 24, 1941, ibid., p. 44.

132, 23 Tom Reiss, "The First Conservative," in *The New Yorker*, October 24, 2005, p. 42.

133, 23 Peter Viereck, *Metapolitics*, Knopf, New York, 1941, p. x.

133, 25 Curzio Malaparte, *The Volga Rises in Europe*, Alvin Redman, London, 1957 (trans. David Moore), p. 21.

133, 28 Loc. cit.

134, 30 Ibid., p. 22.

135, 14 Curzio Malaparte, *Kaputt*, Alvin Redman, London (trans. Cesare Foligno), 1948, p. 121.

135, 18 Ibid., p. 106.

135, 22 Ibid., p. 106.

135, 29 Ibid., p. 124.

136, 6   Ibid., p. 132.

136, 28 Ibid., p. 134.

137, 11 Hans Schwarz van Berk, Introduction to Joseph Goebbels, *Die Zeit ohne Beispiel*, Zentralverlag der NSDAP-Eher, München, 1941, p. 10.

137, 28 Joseph Goebbels, "Mimikry," in *Die Zeit ohne Beispiel*, cit., p. 526.

138, 5 Ibid., p. 527.

138, 8 Loc. cit.

138, 14 Loc. cit.

138, 17 Ibid., p. 531.

140, 4 Secret Service Report in USSR of July 31, 1941, in Kurt Pätzold-Erika Schwarz, *Tagesordnung: Judenmord*, Metropol, Berlin, 1992, pp. 79–80.

140, 15 Felix Hartlaub, note of June–July 1941, in *"In den eigenen Umriss gebannt." Kriegsaufzeich nungen, literarische Fragmente und Briefe aus den Jahren 1939 bis 1945*, edited by G. L. Ewenz, Suhrkamp, Berlin, vol. I, 2002, pp. 79–80.

140, 25 Hans Carossa, "Lebensbericht," in *Ungleiche Welten*, Insel, Wiesbaden, 1951, pp. 110–11.

142, 6 Ibid., p. 123.

143, 10 "Der Reichenau-Befehl," in *Vernichtungskrieg. Verbrechen der Wehrmacht 1941 bis 1944*, published by Hamburger Institut für Sozialforschung, Hamburger Edition, Hamburg, 1996, p. 80.

143, 23 Joseph Goebbels, note of January 24, 1942, in *Tagebücher. Aus den Jahren 1942–43*, edited by L. P. Lochner, Atlantis, Zürich, 1948, pp. 52–53.

144, 2 Patrick Buisson, *1940–1945. Années érotiques*, Albin Michel, Paris, vol. II, 2009, p. 44.

145, 9 Felix Hartlaub, *Aufzeichnungen aus dem Führerhauptquartier* (1942–1945), in *"In den eigenen Umriss gebannt,"* cit., p. 160.

145, 16 Marie Vassiltchikov, note of August 30, 1942, in *Berlin Diaries*, cit., p. 67.

145, 22 Ibid., p. 68.

145, 24 Loc. cit.

145, 25   Loc. cit.

146, 22   Marie Vassiltchikov, note of September 1, 1942, Ibid., pp. 72–73.

147, 2   Marie Vassiltchikov, note of August 31, 1942, ibid., p. 71.

147, 8   Marie Vassiltchikov, note of September 1, 1942, ibid., p. 71.

149, 6   Veit Harlan, *Im Schatten meiner Filme*, edited by H. C. Opfermann, Mohn, Gütersloh, 1966, p. 156.

149, 10   André Gide, note of March 9, 1943, in *Journal*, cit., p. 920.

149, 11   Loc. cit.

149, 12   André Gide, note of April 19, 1943, Ibid., p. 942.

149, 14   André Gide, note of March 12, 1943, ibid., p. 921.

149, 18   Loc. cit.

149, 19   Loc. cit.

149, 22   Loc. cit.

149, 28   Curzio Malaparte, *The Volga Rises in Europe*, cit., pp. 238–39.

150, 4   Ibid., p. 239.

150, 21   Ibid., pp. 240–41.

151, 3   Joseph Goebbels, note of April 9, 1943, in *Tagebücher*, edited by R. G. Reuth, Piper, München, vol. V: *1943–1945. Anhang*, 1999, p. 1920.

151, 12   Joseph Goebbels, note of April 28, 1943, ibid., p. 1925.

151, 13   Loc. cit.

151, 26   Joseph Goebbels, note of April 18, 1943, ibid., p. 1923.

152, 2   Joseph Goebbels, note of April 28, 1943, ibid., p. 1925.

152, 10   Ibid., pp. 1925–26.

152, 19   Communication of the Sovinformburo of April 15, 1943, in *Katyn*, edited by A. M. Cienciala, N. S. Lebedeva and W. Materski, Yale University Press, New Haven and London, 2007, p. 306.

153, 21   Report of the secretary of the Polish Red Cross Kazimierz Skarzynski on his visit to Smolensk and Katyń of April 15–16, 1943 (June 1943, Warsaw), ibid., pp. 312–13.

154, 4   Paolo Monelli, *Roma 1943*, Migliaresi, Rome, 1945, p. 147.

154, 17   Ibid., pp. 147–48.

155, 11   Ibid., pp. 150–51.

155, 15   Norman Lewis, *Naples '44*, Collins, London, 1978, p. 11.

155, 19   Ibid., p. 12.

155, 23   Loc. cit.

156, 14   Heinrich Himmler, *Rede vor den Reichs-und Gauleitern in Posen am 6.10.1943*, in *Geheimreden 1933 bis 1945*, edited by B. F. Smith and A. F. Peterson, Propyläen, Frankfurt-Berlin-Vienna, 1974, p. 164.

156, 18   Ibid., p. 169.

156, 20   Loc. cit.

156, 21   Loc. cit.

156, 26   Loc. cit.

157, 1   Loc. cit.

157, 4   Loc. cit.

157, 5   Loc. cit.

157, 9   Loc. cit.

157, 10   Loc. cit.

157, 12   Ibid., pp. 169–70.

157, 13   Ibid., p. 170.

157, 15   Loc. cit.

157, 18   Loc. cit.

157, 28   Ibid., pp. 170–71.

158, 3   Ernst Jünger, note of October 16, 1943, in *Sämtliche Werke*, cit., vol. III: *Tagebücher (Strahlungen II)*, 1998, pp. 171–72.

158, 5   Ibid., p. 172.

158, 8   Ibid., p. 173.

158, 13   Ibid., p. 174.

158, 17   Loc. cit.

158, 23   Loc. cit.

158, 25   Loc. cit.

158, 28   Loc. cit.

159, 4   Ibid., p. 175.

159, 15   Ibid., pp. 175–76.

NOTES

159, 22 Marie Vassiltchikov, note of October 24, 1943, in *Berlin Diaries*, cit., p. 99.

159, 28 Loc. cit.

160, 6 Loc. cit.

160, 9 Marie Vassiltchikov, note of May 12, 1941, Ibid., p. 50.

160, 11 Marie Vassiltchikov, note of September 8, 1943, ibid., p. 93.

160, 21 Marie Vassiltchikov, note of November 27, 1943, ibid., p. 122.

160, 23 Letter from George Orwell to Noel Willmett, May 18, 1944, in *A Life in Letters*, edited by P. Davison, Penguin Books, London, 2011, p. 232.

161, 9 Loc. cit.

161, 19 Vasily Grossman, *The Road: Stories, Journalism, Essays*, NYRB Classics, New York, 2010 (trans. Robert and Elizabeth Chandler), pp. 153–54.

161, 22 Ibid., p. 157.

161, 24 Ibid., p. 159.

162, 9 Ibid., p. 160.

162, 17 Letter from Louis-Ferdinand Céline to Paul Bonny, September 5, 1944, in *Lettres*, cit., p. 760.

163, 9 Vasily Grossman, *A Writer at War*, edited by A. Beevor and L. Vinogradova, Harvill Press, London, 2005, pp. 341–42.

163, 13 Ibid., p. 335.

163, 28 Ibid., p. 336.

164, 11 Ibid., p. 338.

164, 13 Vasily Grossman, quoted in David Ortenberg, *God 1942. Rasskaz-chronika*, Politizdat, Moskva, 1988, p. 393.

164, 16 Vasily Grossman, *A Writer at War*, cit., p. 342.

167, 7 Charles Baudelaire, *Reliquat du "Spleen de Paris,"* in *Œuvres complètes*, cit., vol. I, 1975, p. 372.

168, 7 Loc. cit.

INDEX

Adorno, Theodor W., 38, 86
Albers, Hans, 148
Alexander, Keith, 27
Alfa, Michèle, 143, 144
Ambor, Cillie, 96, 106
Angel, Anny, 96
Antonescu, Ion, 135
Aristotle, 112, 115
Arletty, 143, 144
Asclepius, 99
Auden, W. H., 4
Augustine, Saint, 43

Báky, Josef von, 147
Balin, Mireille, 143, 144
Bartleby, 37
Baudelaire, Charles,
    48, 167
Bazlen, Roberto, 109
Bébert, 162
Beccaria, Cesare, 33
Beckett, Samuel, 107–109
Bely, Andrei, 108

Benjamin, Walter, 86–87, 95,
    124, 128
Benn, Gottfried, 63
Bentham, Jeremy, 33–34, 41,
    50, 77
Beria, Lavrentiy P., 151
Berzarin, Nikolai E., 163
Bethmann-Hollweg, Theobald
    von, 30
bin Laden, Osama, 10, 13
Bismarck, Otto von, 104
Blanchard, Jean-Pierre, 148
Bogo (alias for Friedrich
    Hielscher), 158–59
Bonny, Paul, 162
Bouthoul, Betty, 10
Bouvard, 19–20, 56
Bracciolini, Poggio, 46
Brasillach, Robert, 94, 116–21
Brecht, Bertolt, 133
Brinvilliers, Marie-Madeleine
    d'Aubray, Marquise de, 158
Brunschvicg, Léon, 112
Buddha, 66

Burckhardt, Jacob, 17–18, 85
Burroughs, William S., 10

Cagliostro, Alessandro, 148
Cantor, Georg, 79
Cardarelli, Vincenzo, 154
Carol, Martine, 143
Carossa, Hans, 140–42
Carpaccio, Vittore, 121
Casanova, Giacomo, 148
Catherine the Great, 147
Céline, Louis-Ferdinand,
    96–97, 100–102, 106, 162;
    see also Destouches, Louis F.A.
Chaitin, Gregory, 78–80
Chalmers, David, 65, 79
Chamberlain, Arthur, 137
Chanel, Coco, 143
Charles XII, 66
Chuikov, Vasily I., 161
Churchill, Winston, 137, 152
Claudel, Paul, 141
Coleridge, Samuel T., 51
Colette, Gabrielle-Sidonie, 121
Cortés, Hernán, 130
Craig, Elizabeth, 101

Dabit, Eugène, 97
Daladier, Édouard, 137
Darwin, Charles, 47
Daumal, René, 58
Deineka, Aleksandr A., 114

Delforge, Lucienne, 106
DeMille, Cecil B., 102, 118
de Staël, Nicolas, 10
Destouches, Louis F. A., 102;
    see also Céline, Louis-
    Ferdinand
Destouches, Lucette, 162
Dönitz, Karl, 155
Dostoyevsky, Fyodor, 37, 44
Doucet, Jacques, 167
Drieu La Rochelle, Pierre,
    100
Dubert, Albert (alias of Arthur
    Koestler), 128
Dürer, Albrecht, 108
Durkheim, Émile, 20–23

Early, Stephen T., 159
Ebermayer, Erich, 93
Einstein, Albert, 129
Elohim, 60
Europa, 89

Faure, Élie, 97, 100–101, 106
Feuchtwanger, Lion, 98
Ficino, Marsilio, 46
Flaubert, Gustave, 43
Fohi, 67
Fragonard, Jean-Honoré, 101
Freud, Sigmund, 20, 61, 96
Froelich, Carl, 148
Frost, Robert, 87, 102

Gadda, Carlo Emilio, 109

Garland, Judy, 147

Garosci, Aldo, 110

Gates, Bill, 63

Gates, Melinda, 63

Gekhman, Efim, 164

Gerratana, Valentino, 126

Ghiha, Vladimir, 136

Gide, André, 116, 130–31, 141, 149

Giraudoux, Jean, 121

Gletkin, 125

Gödel, Kurt, 74

Goebbels, Paul J., 119, 132, 137–39, 143, 147–49, 150–52

Goering, Hermann, 105

Goethe, Johann W. von, 131

Gould, Florence, 143

Grossman, Vasily, 161–64

Guénon, René, 68

Guermantes, Oriane de, 114

Gutsa Voda, Alexandru I., 136

Habsburg, House of, 100

Halévy, Élie, 110–15

Halifax, Edward Frederick Lindley Wood, Viscount, 137

Hammer-Purgstall, Joseph F. von, 9

Harari, Yuval N., 76

Hardy, Daphne, 124, 126

Harlan, Veit, 148

Hartlaub, Felix, 140, 144

Hasan-i Sabbah, 7–8, 10; *see also* Old Man of the Mountain

Heckel, Erich, 107

Hegel, Georg Wilhelm Friedrich, 3, 73

Helvétius, Claude Adrien, 33

Hermes, 72

Herodotus, 42

Hielscher, Friedrich, 158; *see also* Bogo

Hilz, Sepp, 114

Himmler, Heinrich, 118–19, 155–57, 161

Hitler, Adolf, 15, 17, 30, 32, 47, 93, 96–98, 100, 104, 111, 112, 115–17, 119–22, 124, 127, 130, 131, 132–33, 135, 149, 151, 158, 161, 164

Hodgson, Marshall G. S., 7

Hoffmann, E.T.A., 106

Hofmannsthal, Hugo von, 45

Hohenzollern, House of, 100, 145–47

Homais, Monsieur, 43

Hubert, Henri, 20

Hulagu Khan, 8

Hutcheson, Francis, 33

Irrgang, Erika, 96

Isabella d'Este, 148

Isis, 45

Jesus, 139
Joinville, Jean, 9
Jones, Jim, 75
Jünger, Ernst, 98–99, 105–106,
   123–24, 130, 158–59

K., 87
Kafka, Franz, 85
Kamenetzky, Mikhail (Mischa),
   126; see also Stille, Ugo
Kästner, Erich, 148–49
Kerensky, Aleksandr F., 111
Khamenei, Ali H., 13, 27
Khomeini, Ruhollah, 27
Khrushchev, Nikita, 71
Kippenberg, Anton, 98
Kirchner, Ernst L., 107
Kissinger, Henry, 25–28
Klopstock, Friedrich G., 108
Koene, Randal A., 76
Koestler, Arthur, 124–25, 128;
   see also Dubert, Albert
Konstantin of Baviera, Prince,
   145–47
Kosloff, Theodore, 102
Kraus, Karl, 13–14, 124
Kubin, Alfred, 105–106
Kurzweil, Raymond, 74

Lactantius, 44
Lanz von Liebenfels, Jörg, 99–100
Le Vigan, Robert, 162

Léautaud, Paul, 116
Leibniz, Gottfried W. von, 43,
   58, 66–70, 78, 107
Lenin, Vladimir I., 17, 32, 111
Lessing, Gotthold E., 108
Lewis, Norman, 155
Libet, Benjamin, 52
Liebeneiner, Wolfgang, 148
Lindbergh, Charles, 127
Locke, John, 41
Louis XIV, 66
Luchaire, Corinne, 143
Lupu, Constantin, Colonel, 135
Lycophron, 121

Machiavelli, Niccolò, 78
MacLeish, Archibald, 102–103
Malaparte, Curzio, 133–36,
   149–50
Malebranche, Nicolas de, 35,
   85–86
Mandelstam, Osip E., 25
Mann, Klaus, 93, 127
Mann, Thomas, 108
Marc, Franz, 108
Marco Polo, 7–8
Maria-Aldegunde von Hohen-
   zollern, 145–46
Marie Antoinette of Habsburg-
   Lorraine, 98
Marioara, 135–36
Martin du Gard, Maurice, 97,
   98–99, 116

Marx, Karl, 17
Mauss, Marcel, 20, 111, 113, 115
McCullers, Carson, 127
Michelet, Jules, 85
Milch, Erhard, 155
Mill, John Stuart, 42, 50–51
Mithras, 45
Molly, 102
Molotov, Vyacheslav M., 125
Monelli, Paolo, 153–54
Montherlant, Henry de, 97
Morgenthau, Henry, Jr., 160
Muhammad, 40
Mumm, Madeleine de, 143
Münchhausen, Karl F.H.,
    Baron, 147–48
Mussolini, Benito, 102, 111,
    116, 126–27, 154, 155

Napoleon I, 117, 131
Nasser, Gamal Abdel, 12
Nechayev, Sergey G., 5, 33
Nielsen, Michael, 78–79
Nietzsche, Friedrich, 9, 40
Noailles, Marie-Laure de, 143
Nolde, Emil, 107
Nonnus of Panopolis, 121

Odoric of Pordenone, 8
Old Man of the Mountain, 7–9,
    158; see also Hasan-i Sabbah
Orwell, George, 28, 160–61

Pallas, 94
Pannunzio, Mario, 155
Papen, Franz von, 159
Pascin, Jules, 134
Paul, Saint, 20
Pécuchet, 19–20, 56
Pelliot, Paul, 8
Peter of Celle, 35
Peter the Great, 66
Petrov, Colonel, 163
Picard, Max, 109
Pico della Mirandola, Giovanni,
    46
Pintor, Giaime, 126
Pizarro, Francisco, 130
Planck, Max, 129
Plato, 23, 115
Poe, Edgar Allan, 94
Pohl, Otto, 128
Prester John, 9
Priestley, Joseph, 33
Proust, Marcel, 108
Ptolemian, the, 63

Quisling, Vidkun, 127
Qutb, Sayyid, 12–14, 27

Raczyński, Edward B., 152
Rauschning, Hermann, 121–22
Régnier, Henri-François de, 101
Reich, Annie, 96
Reichenau, Walter von, 142–43

Ribbentrop, Joachim von, 119, 125
Rilke, Rainer Maria, 108, 126
Robinson, Edward Arlington, 87
Romanov, House of, 100
Roosevelt, Franklin D., 127, 159–60
Roth, Joseph, 97–98
Rousseau, Jean-Jacques, 17, 117
Russell, Stuart J., 82–84

Sacramozo, 45
Sadat, Anwar, 13
Sade, Donatien-Alphonse-François, Marquis de, 50
Sain, Ludovico, 109
Saint-Simon, Henri de, 17, 22
Salutati, Coluccio, 46
Schmitt, Carl, 105
Schmundt, Rudolf, 143
Scholem, Gershom, 95
Schwarz van Berk, Hans, 137
Searle, John R., 65
Sikorski, Wladislaw, 152
Simenon, Georges, 94
Simon, Sir John Allsebrook, 104
Sironi, Mario, 114
Skarżyński, Kazimierz, 153
Skinner, B. F., 41
Smith, Adam, 83
Söderbaum, Kristina, 148

Sofia, Corrado, 155
Soon, Chun Siong, 52
Sorel, Georges, 111, 112
Speer, Albert, 155
Stahlecker, Franz W., 132
Stalin, Joseph V., 15, 20, 71, 97, 124, 149, 151
Stavisky, Serge Alexandre, 101
Steffin, Margarete, 124
Stille, Ugo (pen name of Mikhail Kamenetzky), 126
Strasser, Otto, 128
Streben, 161
Streicher, Julius, 109
Strindberg, August, 100
Suster, Roberto, 153–54

Taylor, Charles, 44, 46
Tertullian, 44
Thibaudet, Albert, 121
Tiedtke, Irma, 108
Tintoretto, 121
Tocqueville, Alexis de, 34–35
Treskow, Münthe von, 163–64
Trott zu Solz, Adam von, 132
Turing, Alan, 76

Untermeyer, Louis, 102–103

Valentin, Karl, 108
Valéry, Paul, 121, 141

INDEX

Vassiltchikov, Marie (Missie), 131–32, 145, 146–47, 159–60
Vassiltchikov, Tatiana, 160
Verjus, Père Antoine, 66
Viereck, George Sylvester, 132
Viereck, Peter, 132–33
Virgil, 121
Vlasov, Andrej A., 156
Voltaire, 108, 117
Von Neumann, John, 80

Walser, Robert, 37
Walter, Bruno, 95
Wegner, Daniel, 52
Weil, Simone, 23, 48–49, 80–81, 129–30

Wheeler, John A., 78–79
Wigram, Ralph F., 103–104
Williams, Esther, 12
Willmett, Noel, 160
Wittelsbach, House of, 145
Wittgenstein, Ludwig, 24
Woolf, Leonard, 103, 105
Woolf, Virginia, 95–96, 103, 105

Xammar Puigventós, Eugeni, 154

al-Zawahiri, Ayman, 13
Zhukov, Georgy K., 163
Zweig, Arnold, 98
Zweig, Stefan, 97–98

A NOTE ABOUT THE AUTHOR

Roberto Calasso is the publisher of Adelphi Edizioni in Milan and the author of many books. *The Unnamable Present* is the ninth part of a work in progress that currently includes *The Ruin of Kasch*, *The Marriage of Cadmus and Harmony*, *Ka*, *K.*, *Tiepolo Pink*, *La Folie Baudelaire*, *Ardor*, and *The Celestial Hunter* (forthcoming from FSG). He has also written *Literature and the Gods*, *The Forty-nine Steps*, and *The Art of the Publisher*, and is the editor of *The Zürau Aphorisms*, by Franz Kafka.

A NOTE ABOUT THE TRANSLATOR

Richard Dixon lives and works in Italy. His translations from the Italian include *The Ruin of Kasch*, *Ardor*, and *The Art of the Publisher*, by Roberto Calasso, and *The Prague Cemetery* and *Numero Zero*, by Umberto Eco. He is one of the translators of FSG's edition of Giacomo Leopardi's *Zibaldone*.